Where Can Peace Be Found?

Where Can Peace Be Found?

J. Krishnamurti

Shambhala
BOSTON & LONDON
2011

SHAMBHALA PUBLICATIONS, INC.
Horticultural Hall
300 Massachusetts Avenue
Boston, Massachusetts 02115
www.shambhala.com

©2011 by Krishnamurti Foundation Trust, Ltd

Edited by Ray McCoy

Information about Krishnamurti Foundation Trust,
Brockwood Park School, and the Krishnamurti Center
can be obtained by writing to Brockwood Park, Bramdean,
Hampshire s024 olq, uk, or by emailing info@brockwood.org.uk.

9 8 7 6 5 4 3 2 1

First Edition

Printed in the United States of America

♾This edition is printed on acid-free paper that meets the
American National Standards Institute z39.48 Standard.
♻This book was printed on 30% postconsumer recycled paper.
For more information please visit www.shambhala.com.

Distributed in the United States by Random House, Inc.,
and in Canada by Random House of Canada Ltd

Library of Congress Cataloging-in-Publication Data

Krishnamurti, J. (Jiddu), 1895–1986.
Where can peace be found?/edited by Ray McCoy
p. cm.
ISBN 978-1-59030-878-3 (pbk.: alk. paper)
1. Peace. 2. Conduct of life. I. McCoy, Ray. II. Title.
B5134.K751 2010
303.6'6—dc22
2010031810

Contents

Introduction

WHAT IS WRONG WITH US? Are human beings really basically flawed, deeply irrational? From time before we started to measure it, we have had war after war after war, with our neighbor or between tribes, cities, and then nations and alliances of nations. Has there ever been a time when there was not a conflict somewhere on earth? Why, after all our years together in this world of such natural beauty, are we still not in harmony with it? Why, knowing the great potentialities of the human spirit in its most sublime and creative moments, can we not live harmoniously with each other?

Where does the problem begin? In the family, we raise our children to value fairness and to respect others and to care for nature; and we expect our educators and our educational systems to teach the same values. We speak of the equal rights of all human beings to enjoy free and happy lives with decent standards of living and education and ready access to employment. At the same time, we reward competitiveness and assertion of individuality to the point of aggression. We continue to exploit the earth's depleting resources for our ease and luxury, simultaneously preaching the need for conservation and preservation of those resources. This destructive ambivalence is prevalent even in the very institutions we have established to ensure order in society, to protect us from harm, and to inspire and guide our inner growth, which we claim to be our highest and noblest goal.

Political representatives are chosen from candidates who engage in fierce competition for public favor, spending millions on advertising campaigns—and not on benefits for the society they promise to improve. Those who win take their seats in assemblies in which they continue to harangue each other with mere rhetoric, determining policies not by reasoned agreement but by weight of majorities gained partly by manipulating political favors, partly a result of pressure from lobbyists.

In the courts, settlements are not arrived at by impartial examination of the facts directly relevant to the immediate case; decisions are based on whatever precedents already established in law can better be argued pro and con by legal experts. These experts do not work together to find the most equitable and humane solution for both the accused and the accuser; more often they are concerned with punishment for the former or some sort of reward for the other. And prisons, then, are designed not for improvement and education but for punishment and exclusion from society, breeding ever more of the criminality they are established to correct. These systems of government and law, originally based on straightforward concerns for justice and order, have become so swollen with administrative bureaucracies that they are undermined by their own inefficiency.

Even in religion, where the professed intent is unity with a highest principle that embodies peace, forgiveness, compassion for all living things, we find contradictions that beggar belief. Fundamentalists of whatever stripe wage verbal and physical war against those who do not subscribe to their particular interpretation of what their "God" demands in human behavior and values. Every major religion has its history of bloody violence—inquisitions, crusades, fights between sects, persecutions, terrorism—which continues even today. As we proclaim the aim of peace on earth, we bless regimental colors and hang them in our churches, and we fight wars "for God and country." There are actually those, who are not a mere few, who long for the war to end all wars, Armageddon, because that will signal the end of life on earth and they will be Raptured to a heaven created from their imaginations. They alone will be saved, not anyone else.

Clearly, basic human physical needs are for food, clothing, and shelter. The resources of the earth are enough, if shared reasonably and not squandered on armaments and refining military technology, to provide for all of us. Yet, the pursuit of individuals, stimulated by expensive advertising underwritten by businesses at our expense, is to use the resources for ever more comfort and luxury for themselves, not for all. The demands of nations are to control more of the world's resources for their own populations; these resources are seen as a means for power, not for the benefit of all the people of the earth. When we do organize programs to help the poor and disadvantaged, whether at home or abroad, huge amounts are spent on administration and on corrupt payoffs, rather than on providing the goods or services needed. That there is a basic psychological need for freedom from fear is also obvious. Nevertheless, brutal dictators and totalitarian states continue to flourish. However many summit conferences have been held and international accords signed, the fundamental fact is ignored that division breeds conflict, whether the division is within a community or between nations.

What is wrong with us? Can we do anything about it? Can there ever be peace on earth?

In the selections presented here, Jiddu Krishnamurti offers some insights into the reasons for the malaise. The root of the problems is in the self-image that is created by thought. Right exercise of thought has brought great physical benefits through technology, medicine, surgery. But thought, nurtured by human conditioning for countless millennia, has also created fear, authority, divisive beliefs, and insecurity. Above all, thought has created the sense of self, of individuality, that has led to all the props that reinforce that sense and breed competition, greed, isolation, aggression, and self-centeredness and that destroy right relationship between human beings.

Now, we do not use our brains with real creativity because of our conditioning. But Krishnamurti states that freedom from that conditioning is possible and that when freed from conflict and need, human potential is limitless. Recognizing that our consciousness is not individual but common to all humanity, we may, perhaps for the first time, understand the real meaning of cooperation, right relationship, and compassion for all.

During his sixty years of traveling the world giving public talks, Krishnamurti must have encountered most of the divisions that beset society. He saw two world wars, the Korean and Vietnamese conflicts, the tensions of the USSR-USA cold war. He saw the never-ending squabbles over resources, boundaries, and territories. He was well-informed through conversations with statesmen, educators, royalty, and specialists in the sciences, religion, and politics about their concerns and dilemmas. He had hundreds of individual meetings with people from diverse backgrounds, discussing their conflicts in relationship and with themselves.

In 1983, the subject of peace was central to many of Krishnamurti's talks. It was the main theme of four talks at Brockwood Park in England, which form chapters 6, 7, 8, and 10 of this book. These are complemented by chapters 1 and 9 from talks in India, 3 and 4 from talks in California, and 2 and 5 from Switzerland. The chapters are not a series of lectures, so there may seem to be a lack of continuity between them. Krishnamurti described his talks as conversations between himself and those listening. He often began with a reminder of what had gone before. This was helpful for those listening, some of whom had not heard a previous talk, but to avoid unnecessary repetition for a reader who can refer back, these recapitulations have been omitted. Talks are arranged following a sequence that Krishnamurti often uses. He first identifies a topic or problem and investigates its causes. In subsequent talks the subject is explored in depth, seeing the many psychological factors involved and going into the nature of the exploratory process itself.

Krishnamurti usually ended a series of talks in the manner of the last chapter of this book. It is more of a meditation than a conversation, as Krishnamurti places our human concerns in the context of the immensity of life and an unknown dimension that thought cannot touch. Surely, if we can grasp some sense of this, we may begin to see the folly of our history and intelligently put an end to the conflicts, inner and outer, that we have created and endured for so long. Only then can there be peace on earth.

RAY MCCOY
Editor

Where Can Peace Be Found?

I

Putting Our House in Order

THIS IS NOT AN INSTRUCTION, an authority, telling you what to do or what to think. We must look at humanity as a whole. We must question all authority, the physical, the psychological, the authority of war, the authority of governments whether totalitarian or so-called democratic. In investigating, in questioning, in exploring, we must have a brain that is skeptical, doubting, asking questions not from any particular point of view, or belonging to certain tribes, communities, religious or nonreligious. We are going to look together at the world, what it is, as it is, not what we would like the world to be. We are taking the responsibility of observing the actual affairs of the world, as it is.

In the world there is no peace. Though governments talk about peace, there has never been peace in the world. For the last five thousand years historically there have been wars practically every year. Man has killed man in the name of religion, in the name of ideals, in the name of certain dogmas, in the name of God. Man has killed man, and it is still going on. That is a fact. We, inhabiting this unfortunate but beautiful world, seem to be incapable of doing anything about all that. We are tribal-minded, as Hindus, as Sikhs, as Catholics, Protestants, as nationalists. Whether it is Western nationalism or Eastern nationalism, it is a tribal continuity. And that is one of the major causes of war. There are other, economic, social, and linguistic, causes.

To bring about peace in the world requires great intelligence—not sentimentality, not some emotional demonstrations against a particular usage of instruments of war—to understand the very complex situation of the society in which we live. It requires not only humility and objective observation, it also requires that you, as observer, put away all your tribal instincts so that you are no longer a Sikh, a Hindu, a Muslim, a Christian, or a Buddhist but are a citizen of the world. If you hold on to your particular tribalism, to a particular nationalism, to a particular religion, then investigation into whether it is possible to live in this world peacefully, intelligently, sanely, rationally is not at all possible.

Human beings, who have evolved through millions of years, have reached a certain point where we are going to destroy ourselves. Or, we can create a different kind of moral, ethical society. When we explore, as we must if we are at all intelligent and aware of what is going on in the world, we must put aside completely all authority in spiritual matters to investigate freely. So please put aside your ideals, your conclusions, your intellectual theories. This is very difficult to do.

Now let us look at the world. The world is divided into nationalities, geographically, linguistically, religiously. The world is divided into business, spiritual, religious, and nonsectarian interests; it is fragmented. There is war going on in different parts of the world. Society is corrupt, immoral. There is great corruption throughout the world. These are all facts. There is great confusion, disorder, politically, so-called religiously. And we have created this society; each one of us is responsible for the ugliness, the brutality, the violence, the bestiality that is taking place in the world. Unless we put our house in order there will be no order in society. At whatever level of society we live, each one of us has contributed to the confusion, to the immorality, to the insanity of the world. Unless each one of us changes fundamentally psychologically, there will be no peace in the world. You may think that you will have some kind of peace in your mind, but you will never have peace if you do not have order in your daily life. How many take all this seriously? We are too occupied, we have no time. That is an excuse. We have to put our house in order, and we are going to investigate together what the implications of that order are.

Are we aware that we live in confusion, uncertainty, seeking security? One must have security, physical security. Millions are starving. In Europe, unemployment is very great, as it is in America. And those unemployed have no security. Is disorder brought about by each one of us seeking his own particular security? You want security. One must have physical security. And to have lasting, abiding security, you cannot have wars, you cannot have communal conflicts, you cannot possibly belong to a particular system, because then you bring about conflict. Conflict is disorder, whether that conflict is between you and your husband, or you and your wife, between you and the government, between you and your guru.

It is necessary to use words to communicate, but the words are not important. What is important is the content of the word, what lies behind the word. In the struggle to become something, both psychologically as well as outwardly, there is a perpetual conflict in each one of us. In our relationship with each other—sexually, in a family, in a community—conflict exists. To meditate becomes a conflict. To follow somebody becomes a conflict. And that is one of the major causes of disorder, not only in society, but in ourselves. When conflict exists between people, there must inevitably be disorder. We have to see whether conflict *in ourselves* can end. Can conflict, struggle, the pain, the anxiety, the jealousy, the ambition, the enormous amount of suffering human beings have borne, come to an end at the superficial level and deeply?

We are asking whether conflict can end—not in society, because human beings have created society. No god, no extraordinary outside agency has created this society in which we live. We have made it with all the confusion, the injustice, the brutality, the violence, the bestiality; each one of us has brought it about. In a world that is being torn apart, we must be serious, if not for ourselves, for our children, for our grandchildren. It is necessary to be very serious, committed, urgent, not to any theory, not to any ideology, but to find out for ourselves the cause of conflict. Because where you can find the cause that cause can be ended. That is the law.

If there is pain in our body the cause of that pain can be found, and in the finding of the cause there is the remedy and therefore the cause ends. Similarly, if you are really earnest, not playing about with ideas, with speculations, the cause of conflict is very clear. There are many causes, but there is essentially one cause: each one of us is egocentric. In the name of God, in the name of good works, in the name of improving society, we do social work, join parliament and so on, seeking power and money. That is what most human beings want, not only physical power but spiritual power, to be somebody in a "spiritual" world. We all want to find illumination, happiness, so we say we will ultimately achieve that. Time is the enemy of humanity. You have to live *now*. If you say, "I will gradually find out," you will never find out. That is an excuse.

The cause of conflict brings about disorder. So we must first put our house in order, not the physical house, but the psychological world, which is very complex. By the word *psychological* we mean the brain that holds all the content of our consciousness, what you think, what you believe, your aspirations, your fear, your jealousies, your antagonism, your pleasure, your faith, your sorrow. All that is the content of your being; that is the very center of your consciousness. *That* is what you are, not some extraordinary spiritual entity dwelling in darkness, as some believe. You are what you think, what you believe, what faith you follow, your ambition, your name, and so on. That is what you actually are. We are not concerned for the moment with the physical side, because when one understands deeply the psychological nature and structure of oneself then you can deal with the physical activity, sanely, rationally.

So, that is the human condition that has existed for thousands of years. One human being has always quarreled with another, always lived in conflict. Some of the ancient caves portray man fighting man, fighting animals, which is the same thing. It is symbolic, perpetual conflict. We are human beings, and perhaps a few have escaped from conflict, a few people who have gone into this question deeply to understand the nature of conditioning and human condition.

There are those philosophers in the West who say the human condition can never be altered, it can only be modified. They say that we must live in that prison, and that prison can only be made congenial, more respectable, more suitable. They say we must put up with that human condition, which is our anger, our jealousies, our search, our everlasting burden. Modern philosophers have stated that people cannot be changed at all but can only be modified in their brutality, in their violence, in their beliefs, and so on. But we are saying, quite impersonally, emphatically, that the human condition *can* be radically changed if we have the intention, if we observe very clearly without any prejudice, without any direction, without any motive, what we are.

Our condition has been brought about through thousands of years of experience, through various accidents, incidents. That condition has been brought about through the desire to be secure. It has been brought about through fear and the perpetual pursuit of pleasure, and through never-ending sorrow.

We are what we have been as human beings for the last million years more or less. That is our condition. We have created the society. Then the society controls us. So we try to blame the environment, blame education, blame governments, and so on, but we have made all this environment. So we are responsible. So we must understand our conditioning. Our conditioning is to be British, to be French, to be·a Sikh, to belong to some sect. That is our conditioning.

Can we observe our conditioning very closely and clearly? If you say it is not possible to be free from conditioning, you have blocked yourself, you have created a barrier for yourself. Or, if you say that it is possible, that also creates a barrier. Both the positive and the negative become a barrier. But if you begin to investigate, look, observe, then you can discover a great deal.

So we must question what observation is, what looking is. How do you observe yourself? By becoming a monk, by withdrawing from society, by becoming a hermit? Or do you discover what you are through your reactions in your relationship with another? Don't you? Your relationship with your wife, with your husband, with your girlfriend, whatever it is, is very close and very near. In that mirror of relationship you see yourself as you are. Right?

Are you doing this, or just agreeing with words? May I most respectfully ask, are you listening to the words, listening to your own interpretation of the words, or are you actually now, sitting there, observing in the mirror of your relationship with your wife, with your husband, with your neighbor? In that relationship you see your reactions, physical as well as psychological. That is so simple. You start very near to go very far. You want to go very far, but you don't start near at home.

Relationship is one of the most essential things in life. Relationship is a reality. You cannot possibly exist in solitude, alone. *Alone* means "all one," but we are not using the word in that sense. You are solitary and you remain solitary. You think you are an individual and you treat another as an individual. You are two separate entities trying to establish a relationship between two images.

We are trying to find out a way of living, a daily living in which there is no conflict. And to understand the way of that life, we must end conflict, first in ourselves, then in society and so on, to examine, to observe ourselves. So we must comprehend the meaning of that word *observe*. Have you ever observed anything without a motive, without the word, without a direction, just observed? Have you ever observed the ocean, the birds, the beauty of the land, or the beauty of a tree, just to observe, not using the words, "How beautiful"? Have you ever so observed your wife, your children, if you have them? Or do you observe them as belonging to you, as a parent with all your authority? Have you ever observed the evening star, the slip of a new moon, without the word? Observing, you begin to discover your reactions, first your physical sensory reactions and then your psychological reactions.

That sounds very simple; but our brains have become so complex that we hate anything simple. We want it all made complex, theoretical. Begin very simply and begin very near, which is yourself and your relationship. That is the only thing that you have—not your temples, not your beliefs, or whatever you wear. We are human beings. We cannot exist without relationship. It is the most important thing in life. And in that relationship, which is based on image-building, you have an image about her and she has an image about you because you have both lived together for twenty years, for ten days, or one day. You have already created an image. And those *images* have relationship. If I have a wife, I have lived with her sexually, she has nagged me, I have bullied her, I possess her and she likes being possessed. So I have created an image about her, and she has created an image

7

about me. And our relationship is based on those images. When there are images built by thought, built by various experiences and incidents translated by thought and retained as memory, how can there be love? You may love your God—but you don't. You may love your scriptures through fear because you want to be saved. But where there is fear, there is no love.

So the question arises whether it is possible not to create images. You have an image about yourself. Most people have images, but the most intimate image is between you and your wife, or between you and your husband, or your girlfriend. The root of conflict is *there*. It is *there* that you must have order. You cannot put order there; you can only remove disorder, and then there is order. If you remove confusion from your brain, there is clarity.

In relationship, conflict is brought about by thought. Thought is responsible for the image that you have about yourself and about another. Why has thought become so important throughout the world? The world has been divided into Eastern thought and Western thought; but there is no Western thought and Eastern thought. There is only thought, conditioned according to climate, food, clothes, religion, and so on. There is only thought.

Thought is the root of conflict. Thought has brought about disorder in the world by dividing people into nationalities, into religions. Thought has divided the world, and thought has clothed itself in its psyche. Thought has created the most marvelous cathedrals, most marvelous temples, mosques, great architecture and great means of destruction, the atom bomb. Thought has also put all the things in the cathedrals, in the temples, in the mosques, in the places of so-called worship. Thought has invented all that. Without thought you could not exist. Thought, having created the image, then worships the image.

So thought, thinking, is the root of conflict. What can we do without thought? You cannot do without thought; you have to use thought. You use thought to move; you use thought for language. If you are a scientist, you have to use thought. If you are a businessman, you use your thought. You may use thought crookedly, but thought is of neither East nor West; it is thinking. Whether the thinking is that of an authority or your own, it is still thinking.

Thought has brought about most extraordinary things in the world: hygiene, surgery, medicine. Thought has also brought about the atom bomb, the instruments of war. Thought has also divided people as Christians, Hindus, Buddhists, Sikhs. All the so-called sacred books are put down by thought. There is nothing sacred about those books; you may say they are revealed, but it is still the activity of thought. So we have to understand what thinking is, what thought is.

Together we are investigating it, going into it, so you must share, partake in the investigation.

So what is thought? Isn't thinking limited? You will ask why thought is limited when it has created all this, created the society in which we live, created the historical ideals. It is limited because all experience is limited—all experience, whether it is experience of nirvana, the experience of paradise, of sitting next to God, or of achieving. Experience is limited whether it is scientific experience or physical experience or psychological experience. And because it is limited, knowledge is always limited. A scientist never says his knowledge is complete. If you observe historically, the process of science, from the ancient to the modern, is gradually building up knowledge day after day, based on experience. So knowledge and experience are limited. Knowledge is carried in the brain as memory. Memory then responds as thought, so thought is always limited. And that which is limited must invariably create conflict.

If you are thinking about yourself all day long, which most

of us do—about whether you are progressing, whether you are good, whether you look beautiful, whether you are achieving—you are self-centered. When you are thinking about yourself, you are very limited, aren't you? Don't be ashamed, you are limited. It is a fact. And that limitation has been brought about by thought, because you are thinking all day long, in your business, in your science, in your philosophy. You are thinking but always from your center. And that egotistic, egocentric activity is very limited. And therefore you are creating havoc in the world, creating great conflict in the world.

So one asks if there is an instrument other than thought? You have gone into this question of thinking, and looked at the whole problem, and seen how limited it is. On the one hand it creates wars, and on the other it seeks security. War destroys security. Nationalism destroys security. Worshipping destroys the security of humanity. And thought is responsible for all this. And thought is limited. When you really perceive this as an actuality—not as an idea, but actually—then you are bound to ask if there is another instrument than thought. Is there another quality in the brain? Is there a quality that will discover an instrument that is not thought? To find out if there is a different instrument totally untouched by thought, one must be very clear about the nature and the structure of thought, its responsibility, its usage; see where it is limited; and recognize its limitations and move away from those limitations. Then one can begin to ask whether there is a totally different instrument that is not contaminated by thought.

2

Where Can We Find Peace?

THE WORD *FACT* MEANS that which has been done pre-
viously and remembered. What has been remembered is
not the fact, but what has been done in the past is a fact, and
what is happening now is a fact. The future is non-fact; it is
a hope, it is an idea, it is a concept. What actually is a fact is
that which is happening and that which has happened. We are
going to deal together only with facts and not with concepts,
with ideas, with speculations, however philosophical, however
interesting. We are going together to consider the fact of what
we are, the fact of what is happening around us in the world,
and the fact that most of us are concerned with ourselves.

Is it at all possible to live in peace? There is no peace in
the world. There is chaos, disorder, great danger, terrorism,
threats of war. These are all facts. We live every day of our
lives with all the turmoil, with all the labor that people have
to do, with all the problems we have to face. The politicians
talk about peace, the hierarchy of the Catholic church talks
about it, so do the Hindus and the Buddhists and the Muslims,
but actually there is no peace. We must have peace in order to
grow, to flower, to understand, to have time to look around, to
explore into ourselves and see what we can find there. Peace

is not freedom *from* something; freedom between two wars, between two fights, between two problems, or a sense of physical relaxation is not peace. Peace is something much more fundamental, much deeper than the superficial freedom that one may have or that one may think one has.

Is it possible to live in peace both inwardly psychologically, and outwardly? We may want peace, and we may see the necessity of having peace, but we do not live a peaceful life. The world is preparing for war. Ideologies are fighting each other; they do not consider human beings but only the extension of power, so we cannot possibly look for peace from the politicians and governments. That is a fact. Religions have helped to bring about wars. They have tortured, condemned, excommunicated, burnt—and the next moment they talk about peace. Probably only the ancient Buddhists and Hindus have accepted the dictum "Do not kill"; but they do kill. Those religions that are established on books become bigoted, fundamentalist. They become terrorists of the world.

So where does one find peace? Because without peace we are like animals, we are destroying each other. We are destroying the earth, the oceans, the air. None of those groups that are searching for peace have given human beings, you and me, that peace. So where do we find it? Without that fundamental necessity we cannot possibly understand greater things of life.

Let's go into this to find out for ourselves as human beings, without any guide, without any leadership, without any priests, without any psychologists, because they have all failed. Can we have peace in the world and in us? First, can we have peace in ourselves?

The word *peace* is rather complicated. One can give different meanings to it depending upon our moods, depending on our intellectual concepts; romantically, emotionally, we can give different meanings to it. Can we not give different meanings, but comprehend the word and the significance and the depth of that word? It is not merely freedom *from* something, peace of mind, physical peace, but the ending of all conflict. That is real peace not only in ourselves but with our neighbors and with the world, peace with the environment, the ecology. To have deeply rooted peace, unshakable and not superficial, not a passing thing but a timeless depth of peace!

One has sought peace through meditation. All over the world that has been one of the purposes of meditation. But meditation is not the search for peace. Meditation is something far different.

So what is peace, and how can we establish a foundation so that we build on that, psychologically speaking? If we can talk over together what peace is without any bias, without any prejudice, having no conclusions or concepts, then we can go into it; but if you have opinions about peace, what peace should be, inquiry stops. Opinions have no value, though the whole world is run on opinions. Opinions are limited. Your opinion, or my opinion, the opinions of the totalitarians, or the opinions of the church people and governments are all limited. Your judgments and opinions that give values are all limited. When you think about yourself from morning until night, as most people do, that is limited. When you say you are Swiss, or when you are proud to be British as though you are God's chosen people, that is limited.

So opinions are limited. When one sees that clearly, then one does not cling to opinions or the values that opinions have created, because your opinion against another opinion doesn't bring about peace. That is what is happening in the world, one ideology against another ideology—communist, social-ist, democrat, and so on. So please understand that if you are adhering to your opinion and I am sticking to mine, then we shall never meet. There must be freedom from opinion and values so that we are actually not holding back our opinions and using them as axes to beat each other, to kill each other. Opinions are limited and therefore they must inevitably bring about conflict. If you hold on to your limited conclusions, and another holds his limited conclusions, experiences, then there must be conflict, wars, destruction.

If you see that very clearly, then opinions become very superficial, they have no meaning. Don't have opinions, but be free to inquire, and in that inquiry act. The very inquiry *is* action; it is not that you inquire first and then act, but in the process of inquiry you *are* acting.

There must be freedom; it is the very basis of peace. There must be freedom from all the values of opinions so that we can together—actually, not theoretically—see that we have no peace. That is a tremendous demand, because we live on opinions. All the newspapers, magazines, books are based on opinions. Somebody says something; you agree and that is your opinion, too. Another reads another book and forms another opinion. To find out the true meaning of peace, the depth of it and the beauty of it and the quality of it, there must be no bias. Obviously that is the first demand—not that you must have faith in peace, or make it the goal of your life to live peacefully, or search out what peace is from books, from others, but you inquire very deeply into whether your whole being can live in peace.

Action is not separate from perception. When you see something to be true, that very perception is action. It is not that you perceive or understand and *then* act; that is having an intellectual concept and then putting that concept into action. The seeing *is* the action, seeing that the world is broken up by tribalism—the British, the German, the Swiss, the Hindu, the Buddhist, are tribes. See the fact that they are tribes, glorified as nations, and that this tribalism is creating havoc in the world, bringing wars in the world. Each tribe thinks in its own culture opposed to other cultures. But tribalism is the root, not the culture. Observing the fact of that is the action that frees the brain from the condition of tribalism. You see actually, not theoretically or ideationally, the fact that tribalism glorified as nations is one of the causes of war. That is a fact. There are other causes of war, economics and so on, but one of the causes is tribalism. When you see that, perceive that, and see that cannot bring about peace, the very perception frees the brain from its conditioning of tribalism.

One of the factors of contention throughout the world is religion. You are a Catholic, I am a Muslim, based on ideas, propaganda of hundreds or thousands of years; the Hindu and the Buddhist ideas are of thousands of years. We have been programmed like a computer. That programming has brought about great architecture, great paintings, great music, but it has not brought peace to mankind. When you see the fact of that, you do not belong to any religion. When there are half a dozen gurus in the same place, they bring about misery, contradiction, conflict: "My guru is better than yours; my group is more sanctified than yours; I have been initiated, you have not." You know all the nonsense that goes on. So when you see all this around you as an actual fact, then you do not belong to any group, to any guru, to any religion, to any political commitment of ideas. In the serious urgency to live peacefully there must be freedom from all this because they are the causes of dissension, division. Truth is not yours or mine. It does not belong to any church, to any group, to any religion. The brain must be free to discover it. And peace can exist only when there is freedom from fallacy.

You know, for most of us, to be so drastic about things is very difficult, because we have taken security in things of illusion, in things that are not facts, and it is very difficult to let them go. It is not a matter of exercising will, or taking a decision: "I will not belong to anything" is another fallacy. We commit ourselves to some group, to an idea, to religious quackery, because we think it is some kind of security for us. In all these things there is no security, and therefore there is no peace. The brain must be secure; but the brain, with its thought, has sought security in things that are illusory.

Can you be free of that? Are you serious enough to want, or crave, demand, to live in peace? We are asking each other if it is possible to live peacefully for the entire existence of life; not at odd moments, not when one has nothing to do and is captured by television, but to live without a single conflict, without a single problem. Not that there are not problems; there are. But those problems are not being solved, because *we* are the makers of those problems.

It is important to discover for oneself how one's own brain is acting rather than be told by experts, professionals, scientists. The only instrument we have is the brain with its thought. And that brain with its thought has not brought about peace in the world or in oneself. That again is a fact. That instrument, which is thought, has reached the end of its tether.

So where does one explore? And to explore we must be very clear who is the explorer and what is being explored. If I am exploring into what peace is, then I am separate from the thing that is being explored, and so there is division. Where there is division in the inquiry itself, there must be conflict. It is not an intellectual game but rather is an intent to find out the depth of peace and all the great significance of it, the ramifications of it, the expansion of it. It can be found only if we understand from the very beginning that the explorer is the explored. The explorer is not different from that which she or he is exploring.

This is difficult for most of us to accept either intellectually or actually, because our conditioning is so strong. From childhood this division exists: the observer and the observed, the examiner and the examined, the investigator who thinks he is separate from that which he is exploring. This is our conditioning. This is so. This is a fact. And so we live in perpetual conflict because there is division between Catholics, Protestants, Buddhists, Muslims, or Jews. Wherever there is division inwardly or outwardly, there must be conflict. And if you like to live in conflict, that is your affair. Have a good time; enjoy the fun of it and the pain of it. But if you want to discover how to live peacefully, you must understand the basic fact that the explorer is exploring in oneself, not something outside of oneself. The explorer is exploring its own structure, its own activities, its own movements of thought, its own memories. The explorer is all that.

One wonders if you have ever observed that you are a movement of memory. Memory is the faculty to remember, the faculty of time. There is the duration of an incident that might have happened fifty years ago, or yesterday. That incident is over, but the faculty of remembering that incident is memory. And we live on memory, a movement, changing, reacting, constantly shaping itself. We are that. And we think progress is the expansion, the continuation, the heightening of memories, as in a computer.

Memory is the faculty of recalling things that have happened before, which is necessary in the technological and the physical world. When we discover that we are a movement in time, which is the movement of memory, does peace lie in memories? One can remember the days, or the nights, or the mornings when one saw the extraordinary depth and the beauty of peace. That perception, that awareness of a moment has gone, but one remembers that. The remembrance is nonfact; and so we are living in memories that are dead, gone, finished. Please, it is not a depressing or absurd thing for you to turn your back against; see what memory does to us. Memory is my being programmed as a Hindu with all that silly nonsense going on, thinking that my own culture is better than any other culture—because it is about three thousand years old or more, I take great pride. And yours is fairly recent. You are conditioned as the speaker is conditioned—if he is conditioned. The conditioning is memory, non-fact. I stick to my memories, which are dead things, and you stick to your memory as Christian, as Hindu, as an Arab, or Swiss, and so on.

We must have memories. You cannot move if you have no memory. To drive a car, you must have memory. If you are in the technological world, you must be supremely competent in your memories, otherwise you lose your job. But we are talking about the psychological memories of experience, pleasant or unpleasant, painful or delightful. Memories are the conditioning factor. Please see the fact of it, not my explanation of the fact. One of our difficulties is that we like explanations rather than facts. We accept the explanations, the logic, the reasons of journalists and so on explaining why certain governments are behaving in certain ways. The description is not the fact. The painting of a mountain, however beautiful the painting may be, is not the mountain. All the pictures in the museums, some of them extraordinarily beautiful, are not what they represent. You read a novel with all the imaginings, romantic business, sex and so on, written by an excellent, well-known author, but that is not your life. Your life is here. So find out how to live in peace, but not with a method or a system.

To go into it more: what is the cause of conflict, which all of us have? What is the root of it? What is the root of all problems, whether problems of meditation, problems of relationship, political or religious problems? The root meaning of that word is something thrown at you, something hurled at you. If you respond to that thing called *problem* from your memories, your memories will not answer the problem, because your memories are not alive, they are dead. Understand the significance of this! We live with dead things. There is a picture of my son, brother, aunt, uncle, or whatever on the mantelpiece. The person is dead and gone. He can never come back; physically he is gone, incinerated or buried. But I have that picture, the constant remembrance of something that has gone. And I keep up that romantic, illusory memorial relationship. So my brain is never clear. It is always functioning within the field of memory. And to live with a sense of great abundance, flowing peace, there must be freedom from the past, which is memory; not freedom from the memory of how to get home, or how to speak a language, but from the brain holding on to dead things as memory.

What is the function of the brain? Inquire into yourself sanely, not neurotically, not self-centeredly. If you are self-centered and inquiring into that, you will still condition the brain to be self-centered. So what is the function of the brain? One can see one of its major functions is to live in the physical world, is to arrange the physical world. But that very brain has brought about chaos in the world. The activity of the brain is the root and the beginning of thought; that is the instrument with which we operate thought. That is the major function of the brain. And that function has created extraordinary havoc, disorder in the world. That very brain has also brought about health, communication, and medicine, great surgery. To communicate from India to California takes a few minutes. Of course it is not as rapid as thought, but technology is galloping at a tremendous speed. And that very technology is creating havoc in the world, too, like the computer, like the atom bomb. Two great powers—I don't know why they are called great powers, they are two idiotic powers—are talking about killing each other with the latest bombs. That is what thought has done as one of the faculties of the brain. And also thought has created the marvelous, magnificent cathedrals and all those things that are inside them. They are not God-given or something mysteriously brought about. All the dressings and the trappings of the priests are the result of thought, copying the ancient Egyptians and so on. See what thought is doing in the world. And we, our brain, which has evolved through time, endless generation after generation, is doing all this. Creating and destroying! And we accept this way of living. We have never challenged ourselves to find out why we live as we do in this chaotic world outside and with inward chaos. We never realize that to have order in the world outside there must be order in us. Our own house is the most important thing to clean up first, not the world around us. Certain things are necessary—like an organization not to kill whales, to protect nature, and not to destroy the earth by governments, for which we are all responsible, seeking more and more oil!

So what is the deep fundamental function of the brain? Ask yourself this question. If you ask yourself that question, not depending on what others say, on their ideas and suppositions and theories, when you begin to inquire very, very deeply into the fundamental activity—which is essential—what is it doing, what does the brain want? Is it just survival? Just to live in this perpetual conflict, division, quarrelling? Is it to act and function within its own conditioning? Is it to live perpetually in some form of illusion and therefore always be slightly neurotic, unbalanced, as most people are? If it is none of these things, which obviously it is not, then what is its function?

Please, you are asking this question of yourself. Do you really want to find out what the deep function of the brain is and whether the brain is different from the mind, or if they are both the same? When the brain is unconditioned, thoroughly, completely, then the mind can act upon the brain. One has to be very clear where its physical activities must necessarily exist, the technological, physical earning a livelihood, and so on. That is one of its great activities. But if the other activity is contrary to that, then there must be perpetual imbalance.

The first thing is to find out if the brain can be unconditioned. We were discussing in New York two months ago whether the brain cells, which are conditioned, can bring about a mutation in themselves, not genetically, but in living. In daily living, can there be a mutation in the brain cells? If not, we are condemned forever to live in our conditioning and therefore in perpetual conflict, and therefore with no peace at all.

3

Thought and Knowledge Are Limited

W E SHOULD LOOK AT THE WORLD as it is, the whole world, not a particular part of the world or a particular group. We will not be concerned for the moment with our own particular problems, of which we have many, but will look at the whole world, the whole earth upon which human beings are living.

This world in which we live has been broken up into various forms of linguistic, nationalistic, patriotic, religious divisions. There is the Buddhist religion, the Hindu, the Tibetan, the Muslim, the Christian, and also the recent religion of communism, Marxism. There are totalitarian states in certain parts of the world where there is no freedom to think what you like, to do what you like. Wars are going on in different parts of the world. Human beings are killing each other for some idealistic, nationalistic, or racial division. Human beings are slaughtered by the latest machinery of war.

We are not judging or looking at all this from any prejudice or from any bias; we are looking at it together to find out for ourselves why this is happening, why there is so much misery in the world, so much confusion, great uncertainty. The world is becoming more and more dangerous to live in.

In the world there are a great many institutions, foundations, organizations, little groups with their particular leaders,
their gurus with their absurdities. There are threats of various
kinds. Each group, each community, is separating itself from
others. This is what is actually happening all over the world,
and more so in this part of the world where each one wants to
do what he likes, to fulfill himself, to express, to assert.

When one looks objectively, without any bias, at all the ter-
ror, the suffering, the inefficient management of governments,
each country accumulating the instruments of war, one must
ask who is responsible for this human problem, this great
crisis. One can easily say that it is the environment, society,
mismanagement, and so on, but can we look at all this—not
as Americans or Hindus or a particular group, but seriously,
objectively—to find out together for ourselves without being
told, without being instructed or informed, who is responsible
for all these terrible things that are going on? Society, in which
we all live, is corrupt, immoral, aggressive, destructive. This
society has been going on in primitive or modified form for
thousands of years upon thousands of years, but it is the same
pattern being repeated. These are all facts, not opinion or judgment. Facing this enormous crisis, one asks not only what one
is to do but also who is responsible, who has brought the chaos,
the confusion, the utter misery of humanity.

Is the economic crisis, the social crisis, the crisis of war, the
building of enormous armaments, the appalling waste, outside
of us? Inwardly, psychologically, we are also very confused;
there is constant conflict, struggle, pain, anxiety. We are together taking a journey into the whole structure that mankind
has created, the disorder that human beings have brought about
in this world. There is misery, chaos, confusion outwardly in
society; and also inwardly, psychologically, in the psyche, the
consciousness, there are pain and struggles.

What are you going to do about all this? Turn to leaders,

better politicians? This one isn't good, but the next one will be better; and the next one still better. We keep this game going. We have looked to various so-called spiritual leaders, the whole hierarchy of the Christian world. They are as confused, as uncertain, as we are. If you turn to the psychologists or the psychotherapists, they are confused like you and me. And there are all the ideologies: communist ideologies, Marxist ideologies, philosophical ideologies, the ideologies of the Hindus and the ideologies of those people who have brought Hinduism here, and you have your own ideologies. The whole world is fragmented, broken up, as we are broken up, driven by various urges, reactions, each one wanting to be important, each one acting in his own self-interest. This is actually what is going on in the world, wherever you go. In the most poverty-ridden villages in India or among the most highly sophisticated people in the West, it is the same issue, the same problems. There is poverty, hunger, man against man, one ideology against another ideology. This is the actual fact.

What are we all going to do about it? Is each one of us responsible? Please, do ask this question of yourself.

Do you look to another to instruct you, to guide you, to tell you what to do? There are people who will do all that; and through the centuries neither the so-called spiritual leaders nor so-called statesmen have helped mankind to bring about a different world. So where will you look? All leaders are like the led, and the various gurus are like their disciples. All the leaders in the world have failed, not only in this generation but in the past generations. Leaders have not helped. Statesmen throughout the world have not brought about a different society, put an end to wars. So where will you look? The priests have failed; organizations, institutions have lost their meaning. Foundations, little groups, self-assertive little gatherings have not helped to bring about a change in humanity. People have not changed, though we have evolved from the animal to the present so-called civilized human being. After a long evolution psychologically, we are still rather primitive. That is a fact. So where will you look for help? Can anyone help?

We have been trained, educated, to run away from all these problems, to seek some kind of comfort, some kind of an answer from somebody else. All the religious books cannot possibly answer this question. Nobody on earth or in heaven is going to help you. You can pray, and that to which you pray is the creation of your own thought. One wonders if you actually face this fact. God is the creation of thought, of man, out of his fear, out of his anxiety, desire for comfort, seeking somebody to help. Thought has created this entity called *God*. That is a fact.

Each one of us is responsible for all this, for any kind of war that is happening in the world, because in ourselves we are divided, fragmented; in ourselves we are nationalistic, patriotic. Each one of us wants fulfillment immediately. We are encouraged by the psychologists to fulfill whatever desire there is. Each one of us is responsible, as long as we are violent, as long as we are in disorder, as long as we are trying to fulfill our own particular competitive, aggressive, brutal, angry, violent urges. As long as we are all this, our society is going to be that. We have created this society, and nobody else.

If you are not too self-centered, occupied with your own particular little problems, desires, pleasures, and are aware, not merely intellectually but are observing the things that are taking place, you must be greatly concerned not only for yourself, but for your children, for the future. What is the future of mankind? is a fundamental question that one must ask, not of someone else but of oneself. How has all this been brought about? And what can each one of us do? What is our action, facing the outward crisis and in ourselves?

To find out, one must be free to look, free from all bias, free from all conclusions. The word *conclusion* implies to conclude, to shut down. We conclude a peace; that means the ending of a certain war. To conclude an argument means to end that argument. So, without any conclusion, without any bias whatsoever, if you look at all this, is it thought that is responsible?

Thought has created the extraordinary world of technology, the inventions, communications, the subtle surgeries, medicine. That is a fact. Thought also has created national divisions, hoping in divisions to find security. If you believe in a particular form of religious ideology, that again is the activity of thought. Not only the political divisions that exist in the world, the religious divisions that exist in the world, but also the marvelous architecture, the great cathedrals of the world and the small churches and all the things that are in the churches and the cathedrals, in the temples and mosques throughout the world, are all produced by thought. The rituals, the ceremonies, the costumes of the priests are all the result of thought.

You are thought, aren't you? You are memories, remembrances; with your tendencies you are the past, which is the accumulation of experience and knowledge. It is a simple fact that you are memories, subtle, sublimated, crooked, one thought suppressing another thought. Thought is utterly responsible for all the things that are going on in the world.

Please examine it; do not deny it or say it is right or wrong. Look at it. Have the patience, courage, and be serious enough to look at it. It is easy to say no or yes, but see the truth that the actuality of what you believe is the activity of thought. Your relationship with another is the remembrance of thought. So you are basically a bundle of memories. You may not like the fact, you may reject it, but that is a fact. If you had no memories of any kind, you would be in a state of amnesia, in a state of utter blankness, vagueness, vacancy. This is a hard thing to face.

So thought is responsible for the religious, political, personal, racial divisions, the wars that are going on between the Jews and the Arabs, between various religious groups. It is all the result of thought. See the fact, the truth of it. It is not a superstition, some exotic idea imposed upon you. If you see the truth of it, objectively, impersonally, without any bias whatsoever, then the question arises: can thought be aware of itself?

If it is a fact—and it is—that thought has brought about this disorder in the world, then who is to put order in the world? Or in oneself? Apart from nature, the world outside is the result of *our* activity. Our activity of thought has brought about disorder in ourselves, and so the society is in disorder. Unless we put order in our own house, there will be no order in society, in our relationship. That is a fact!

We have separated thinker and thought. Have you observed that the thinker is always correcting thought, controlling it, denying it, shaping it, putting it into a mold—this is right, this is wrong, this should be, this must not be? We think the thinker is separate from thought, so there is a division between the thinker and the thought. That is clear. There is a division between the thinker who is the past and the thought that is taking place now. That is the basis of fragmentation in us.

We are asking why, in human beings, inwardly, psychologically, there is this division, as there is division, separation in the world. Why is there this fragmentation of human beings into Christian, Jew, and so on? What is the root of this fragmentation? The root of it is the division between the thinker and the thought. Is that division real or fictitious? There is no thinker apart from thought. The thinker is the past, so is thought. Thought is the result or the response or the reaction of memory. Memory is the result or reaction of knowledge. Stored in the brain, knowledge is experience. In the scientific world, in the technological world, the inward psychological world, there is knowledge, experience, memory, and the response of that is thought. That is a fact. And knowledge is always incomplete, whether in the present or in the future or in the past. There is no complete knowledge about anything. There can never be. Even the scientists, biologists, and archaeologists admit that knowledge is limited.

Where there is limitation of knowledge, there must be limitation of thought. When you say, "I am a Christian," it is limited. When you are thinking about yourself, your problems, your relationships, your sexual pleasures and fulfillment, that is very, very limited. And thought is limited. It can invent the limitless, but that is still the product of thought. It can invent heaven or hell or whatever, but it is still limited. Where there is limitation, there must be fragmentation.

We are talking about our daily life. When I say I am a Hindu or a Catholic, it is limited. Where there is limitation, there must be division, conflict. Where there is division, there must be disorder. And we live in disorder.

In the old world, there was order of some kind, because they followed certain traditions. In the modern world, tradition is thrown overboard, and there is nothing left, so you do what you want to do. And each one of us in this world is doing what he wants to do, doing "his thing." And look at what chaos it is bringing about—political lobbies, each individual following his or her own particular inclination, religious or otherwise, the immense propaganda that goes on in the name of religion, in the name of this or that.

So, in our actual daily relationship, intimate or otherwise, there is fragmentation. The wife or the girl or the boy or the husband follows his or her own inclinations, desires, sexual demands. You know all that. Two separate entities may have a sexual relationship, but otherwise they may actually have no relationship at all. Each one is pursuing his own ambition, his own fulfillment, his own urges, inclinations, obstinacy. And we call this conflict relationship. That relationship, which is not relationship at all, has brought about division. You may hold the hand of another, embrace another, walk together, but inwardly you are separate from the other. That is a fact. Do face it. And so there is perpetual conflict.

So, one asks if it is possible to live in relationship with another without conflict. Relationship is the greatest thing in life. You cannot live without relationship. You may withdraw from all relationship, finding that relationship is painful, that you are always living in struggle, conflict, possessing and not possessing, jealous. There are those who withdraw from all relationship, like the hermits, the monks, those who live in solitude whether in the great mountains of India or in this country, but they are related. They cannot possibly escape from having some kind of relationship.

So is it possible, as it is necessary, to live in relationship without a single shadow of conflict? Please, *you* are asking this question. This is an important question, a deep, fundamental question. If you cannot live in relationship with each other without conflict, then you will create a world that is full of conflict.

What is the cause of this conflict, of this disorder in ourselves, in our relationship, and the cause of the disorder that exists outside of us? What is the actual fact of relationship? The fact, not romantic, sentimental stuff, but the actual fact, the brutal fact of it. Because if one does not really understand the beauty, the depth, the vitality and the greatness of relationship, we do make a mess of our lives.

Is our relationship based on memory? Is it based on remembrances? Is it based on past incidents accumulated as various images, pictures? If it is remembrance, if it is various images, then all that is the product of thought. Then one asks: is thought love? Do please ask this question of yourself, not because I am prompting you. Is accumulated knowledge of each other love? That knowledge must always be limited and therefore that very knowledge is the root of conflict. Is that love? Not love of some romantic idea, love of God, but love between human beings, a friendship, a sense of communication, communion, nonverbal and verbal.

So, is it possible to live with another without a single image, without a single remembrance of the past that has given you pleasure or pain? Look at it.

Is it possible not to build images about another? If you build images about the other, which is knowledge, then it is perpetual division. Though you may have children, sex, and so on, it is fundamentally division. Like the Arab and the Jew, the Christian and the Muslim, and so on, where there is division, there must be conflict. That is a law. Can I, can you, can each of us have a relationship in which there is no conflict whatsoever? Go into it.

This is part of meditation; not all the silly things that are going on in the name of meditation. This is meditation: to find out, to probe into oneself to see whether it is possible to live with another happily, without domination, without suppression, without the urge to fulfill—all that kind of childish stuff—to live with another without any sense of division. Division must exist as long as thought is in operation, because thought is limited, because knowledge is limited. And in that division there is great pain: anxiety, jealousy, hatred; "me first and you after."

Observe the fact that you are divided from another, like two parallel lines never meeting, except perhaps sexually; two separate railway tracks, each pursuing the other in their own way, clinging to each other. All that brings about great misery in one's life. To observe the fact that you are divided, delve deeply into the fact. When you say "my wife," "my girlfriend," look at the words, feel the words, the weight of the words, the weight of the word *relationship*. To weigh the word means to hold the word.

Observe the whole implication of relationship, not only human relationship, but also relationship with nature. If you lose relationship with nature, you lose relationship with people. To observe, observe without any bias; look at it to feel the division. When you so observe, that very observation is like a tremendous light put on the word *relationship*. To watch means to watch without any direction, without the word, without any motive, just to watch all the implications, the content of that word *relationship*. Live with that word, even for an hour, for ten minutes, for a day, and find out! To live with it, to so observe, means to give your complete attention to that. When you attend completely, the obstacles, the divisions, disappear. It is like bringing great energy to something that has been broken. It is possible to live without a single conflict.

But you may live without conflict, and the other may not. You may have understood, gone into the question of relationship, shed tears, laughed, seen the humor of it, weighed the word, lived with the word. You may have gone into it and comprehended it, seen the truth of it, but the other may not have. Your wife or your husband may not, or your girlfriend may not. Then what is your relationship with the other? What is the relationship between a very intelligent person and a stupid one? Suppose you are very intelligent, in the ordinary sense of that word for the moment (which is not intelligence at all). Suppose you are very intelligent, then what is my relationship to you if I am dull, rather stupid, clinging to my own prejudices, obstinate in my own opinions? What is your relationship to me then? Go into it, please look at it. Will you tolerate me, be sympathetic with me, be kind to me? That means there is still the division.

Suppose you have ended division. Does that imply that there is the sense of love? What if you have that quality, that perfume, and I have not, and I am your wife or husband or your father, mother?

It is strange in this country that the fathers and mothers do not count anymore. They are packed away in some place, sent to an old women's home or men's home. In Asia, where there is no Social Security, the father and the mother live with their children. That is why they say they must have children. That is one of the reasons why the population is growing so tremendously—when the parents are old, the children will look after them. Here, all that is gone. Please consider all this when you talk about relationship with nature and how we are destroying the world, polluting the air, the earth, the sea, destroying the beauty of the earth. And consider the beauty of relationship, to live completely at peace with one another.

Can there be peace in this world? Not in heaven—that is an old, old, traditional disease. Can there be peace between human beings whatever their color, their race, their language, their so-called culture? To find that peace, there must be peace between you and another, between you, your wife, your children. Can there be peace? Which means no conflict. For no conflict, there is something far greater than the activity of thought; which does not mean that you become lazy, a vegetable. On the contrary, you have tremendous energy, not to do more mischief but to live rightly.

4

War Is a Symptom

HUMANITY HAS EVOLVED probably a million years more or less biologically, and has always been crying for peace on earth, but there is no peace in the world. Without peace we cannot possibly flower, we cannot evolve. To see the extraordinary depth of life, the beauty of it, the immensity of all living things, one must have peace. And that peace is denied wherever there is poverty.

In this country, although this society is affluent, there is a great deal of poverty. As you go farther east, poverty increases, in Africa, the Middle East, India, and so on. No nationalistic government can ever solve poverty because it is a global problem. It is a problem of the whole world, not of a particular government, whether it is totalitarian, Marxist, or so-called democratic. If you have lived in a country where there is immense poverty, you have seen the effect of it, the degradation, the utter slavery of it, the brutality. Poverty is not only outward; there is poverty of the mind, and that poverty of the mind is not enriched through books, through institutions and organizations and foundations or forums. The mind is enriched when one understands the whole existence of oneself and one's relationship to the world at large.

Religions have not encouraged or brought about peace in the world. The Christian world talks about peace on earth, but religions have divided man. I do not know how many religious groups there are in this little village, probably dozens of institutions and foundations each trying to tell the other fellows what to do. Religions have prevented peace. Religions throughout the world have prevented humanity from having right relationship with humanity. There have been five thousand years of war. This is historically stated, and we are still going on with wars, killing each other. Perhaps in the beginning you killed with a club; now you can vaporize people by the millions. We have not evolved inwardly, psychologically, and as long as we are primitive psychologically, our society will be equally primitive.

Can there be peace on this earth? Is it at all possible to live peacefully, not only in oneself, but without outward conflict? Or is mankind condemned forever to live in conflict, in wars? It is very important to ask this question of ourselves, not of another. Is there a way out of all this? Certainly not through religions or cultures as they are, nor through political organization, whether democratic or totalitarian or Marxist, nor through divisions of nationalities. We do not ask whether governments can bring about peace, because governments are created by what we are. They have been structured, put together, by our own demands.

So, one asks if it is possible to have peace on this earth? This has been a cry for centuries; long before Christianity came into being. The Buddha was talking about peace 2,500 years ago, and we are still talking about it. Realizing all this, what is one to do? So-called individual efforts to live in peace do not affect the whole world. You may live peacefully, quietly, in this lovely valley, not be too ambitious, not too corrupt, not too competitive. Perhaps you can get on with your wife or your husband, but will that affect the whole of human consciousness? Or is the problem much greater, much more profound?

To find that out, we have to think together. It is like two old friends sitting in the shade of the trees and talking about all this, not merely intellectually but because their hearts are disturbed. They are greatly concerned about what is happening in the world and what is happening to themselves. We are like two old friends who have an amiable conversation; not convincing one another, not stimulating one another, not sticking to opinions and judgments and conclusions, so we can think together, observe together. We observe the trees, the skies, the birds, and the astonishing beauty of the mountains, and ask, "Can we live peacefully, not only you and I, but the rest of humanity?" Because this earth is ours, not American or Irish or English or French. It is our earth, but we are its guests. We have to live here peacefully.

What is the cause of all this? If one can find the cause, then the effect, the symptom can end. War is a symptom. The cause is very deep, complex. When you can find the cause of a disease, that disease can be cured. Why have human beings become like this? They are so thoughtless, concerned only with themselves, and nothing matters except their own desires, their own urges, their own impulses, their own ambition, their own success in the world. Psychologically, inwardly, they want to be somebody, become somebody. But is there psychological evolution at all? That is, is there a becoming at all, psychologically, inwardly achieving, from *what is* to *what should be*, from misery to some form of happiness, from confusion to enlightenment?

To go from *that which is* to *what should be* is becoming. Becoming implies time. Each one trying to become something psychologically may be the same movement as, physically, for a priest to become a bishop, for a clerk to become an executive. It is the same movement, the same wave, brought over to the psychological realm. In all religions and in the psychological world, the idea of change is to become: I am confused; I must change this confusion to become clear. I quarrel with my wife;

the change to stop that, or to end that, is to move from the violence to nonviolence. That is, there is always the attempt to be
something that one is not.

It is a lovely morning, the sun is warm, and the shadows
are many, and the shadows matter as much as the sun. There
is great beauty in the shadows, but most of us are concerned
with light, enlightenment, and we want to achieve that. This
very psychological achievement may be one of the factors of
conflict in life.

Let's examine what it is to become. Is that the fundamental cause of division? Division must exist as long as there is the
psyche, the self, the "me," the ego, one person, separating himself from another. This has been a long history; this is what the
human condition is. We have been trained, educated, to accept
both religiously and economically, and so on, that we are individuals, separate from the rest of humanity, separate from each
other. Is that so? Are we really individuals? This is the tradition,
this is what all religions have said, but together we are going to
examine whether we are really individuals at all.

See all the implications of it before you deny or accept. Now
you accept that it is your condition to be an individual, free to
do what you want to do. The totalitarians deny this; they say
you are just a cog in the whole social structure. We are questioning whether psychological becoming may be an illusion,
and also whether we are separate psychologically.

You suffer, you are confused, you are unhappy, you are anxious, uncertain, insecure. You may have security outwardly,
but even that is becoming more and more uncertain. There are
millions unemployed in this country and in England; and the
unemployment in India is something not known. This unemployment is causing great misery, unhappiness, and conflict,
hatred.

We are questioning whether we are individuals at all, or are
like the rest of humanity. The rest of humanity are unhappy,

sorrow-ridden, fearful, believing in some fantastic romantic nonsense. They go through great suffering, uncertainty, like us. And our reaction, which is part of our consciousness, is similar to the other's. This is an absolute fact. You may not like to think about it, you might like to think that you are totally separate from another, which is quite absurd, but your consciousness—which is you, what you think, what you believe, your conclusions, prejudices, your vanity, arrogance, aggression, pain, grief, sorrow—is shared by all humanity. That is our conditioning whether we are Catholic or Protestant or whatever we are.

Your consciousness is your essence, what your life is. That is the truth, so you actually share the rest of humanity; you are the rest of humanity. That you are humanity is a tremendous thing to realize. You may believe in a certain form of savior, and another believes in another form of ideology, and so on, but belief is common to all of us. Fear is common to all of us; the agony of loneliness is shared by the rest of humanity. When one realizes the truth of that, *becoming*—that is to change from *what is* to *what should be*—has a totally different meaning.

It is your daily life whether you live here or in New York or other big cities, or all the cities of the world. It is our life. We have to understand that, and not from another. We have to examine the facts of our life; to look at ourselves as we look at ourselves when we comb our hair or shave, objectively, sanely, rationally, without any distortion, seeing things as they are, and not be frightened or ashamed, but observe.

All their lives people have tried to change from *what is* to *what should be*. They know violence, disorder, very well, and have tried to change that disorder and violence, to change from violence to nonviolence, from disorder to order. Is nonviolence a fact or just an imaginary conclusion, a reaction from the fact of violence? If I am violent, I project the idea of nonviolence, because that is part of my conditioning. I have lived in disorder, and I try to seek order, to change *what is* to *what should be*. That is part of becoming. And that may be the cause of conflict.

You are examining it. It is being expressed in words, but you are also observing not only the words but the fact.

Can violence end? Not become nonviolent! Can envy, greed, fear end? Not *become* free from that. That is the question. First realize what we are doing—*what is* is to become the ideal, which is *what should be*. But the ideal is nonexistent, is non-fact, and *what is* is a fact. So let us understand *what is* and not the *idea* of nonviolence, which is absurd. Nonviolence has been preached by various people in India. This is our tradition, this is our conditioning; this is our attempt to become something. And we have never achieved anything. We have never become nonviolent. Never.

So let us examine carefully whether it is possible to end that which is, to end disorder or violence. End, not become something. The becoming implies time. This is very important to understand. Let's understand whether it is possible to end *what is*, not to change *what is* into what we would like it to be. Take the question of violence, or if you prefer, disorder. Both are the same, so it doesn't matter which you take. Violence is inherited from beyond all time, from the animal, from the ape. We have inherited it. That is a fact. We are violent people. Otherwise we would not be killing anybody, we would not be hurting anybody, we would not say a word against anybody.

We are by nature violent. Now what is the meaning of that word? Hold that word, feel the weight of that word, the complications of that word. It is not merely physical violence, the terrorist throwing bombs. Terrorists want to change society through various forms of disturbance and bombing and so on, but they have never changed society. And there are the terrorists who do it for the fun of it. Violence is not only physical but much more psychological. Violence is conformity, because to conform to something is to imitate, not to understand *what is*.

Violence must exist as long as there is division outwardly and inwardly. Conflict is the very nature of violence.

Now how do you end it? How do you end the whole complex problem of violence? I understand very well that to become nonviolent is a part of violence, because I have projected nonviolence from violence, and that projection is really illusion. So I have rejected that concept, that idea, that feeling that I must become nonviolent. There is only the fact of violence. Do not ask me how to end it. Let's look at it. The moment you ask what to do, or how to do it, you put another as your guide. You make him or her your authority, and therefore friendship ceases.

So let's together look at it. Let's observe what violence is, look at it, give attention to the fact, not escape from it, not rationalize it. We do not say, "Why shouldn't I be violent, it is part of myself." If that is part of ourselves, we will always create wars of different kinds, wars between me and my wife, killing others, and so on. Look at it without conflict. Look at it as though it is not separate from you. This is rather difficult. Violence is part of you. You are violent, like you are greedy. Greed is not separate from you. Suffering is not separate from you. Anxiety, loneliness, depression: all that is you. But our tradition, our education, has said that you are separate from that. So where there is separation, where there is duality, there must be conflict. It is like the Jew and the Arab: conflict, division between two great powers. So, it is you. You are that. You are not separate from that. The analyzer is not different from the analyzed.

You observe the tree, the mountain, your wife and your children. Who is the observer, and who is the observed? Is the observer different from the tree? Of course he is different—I hope! The observer is different from the mountain. The observer is different from the computer. But, is the observer different from anxiety? Anxiety is a reaction; it is put into words as *anxiety*, but the feeling is you. The word is different, but the word is never the thing. The thing is the feeling of anxiety, the feeling of violence. The word *violence* is not that feeling. So watch carefully that the word does not entangle your observation. Because our brain is caught in a network of words. When I say I am an American, I feel very proud; as when I call myself a South African or a Zulu. So we must be very careful that the language does not condition our thinking.

Observe the feeling without the word. If you use the word, you strengthen the past memories of that particular feeling. There is the act of observation in which the word is not the thing and the observer is the observed. The observer who says "I am violent" *is* violence. So, the observer is the observed, the thinker is the thought, the experiencer who says "I must experience nirvana or heaven" is the experience, the analyzer is the analyzed, and so on. So look at the fact of that feeling without a word, without analyzing it. Just look. That is, be with it. Be with the thing as it is. Which means you bring all your attention to it. Analyzing, examining, is all a waste of energy; whereas if you give your total attention, which is to give all your energy to the feeling, then that feeling has total ending.

I am not stimulating you, I am not telling you what to do. You yourself have realized that nonviolence is non-fact, that it is not real. What is real is violence. You yourself have realized it. You yourself have said, "Yes, I am violent, I am not separate from the violence." The word separates, but the fact of the feeling is me. "Me" is my nose, my eyes, my face, my name, my character. That is me. I am not separate from all that. When you separate, you act upon it, which means conflict. When you are that, are not separate from that, you have fundamentally erased the cause of conflict.

So, I have learned a great phenomenon, which I have never realized before. Before I have separated from my feelings as though I was different from feeling. Now I realize the truth that I am that. Therefore I remain with it. And when you remain with it, hold it, you are out of that; which gives you tremendous energy. And that energy dissipates, ends violence completely. Not just for a day, not only while you are sitting there, but it is the end of it.

One of our problems is that, from time beyond time, mankind has lived with fear of various kinds: fear of ending, death; fear of not gaining; fear of being a failure in life; fear of losing a job; fear of darkness; fear of what the public will say; fear I might lose my wife or husband; fear of being dull. When I see someone bright, intelligent, capable, alive, I am jealous; that is part of fear. We must understand the nature of fear and the structure of fear; because out of fear we have created gods. If we are not afraid at all, we are the most liberated people on earth. Then we do not want gods; we are gods ourselves.

To understand the nature of fear, we must very carefully examine time. Time is fear. I am afraid of tomorrow; I am afraid of what has happened two years ago. Two years ago is the past; the past is time. Being afraid of what might happen tomorrow is part of time. I have a job, but I might lose it; that is time. So, we must go very carefully into what time is, and understand it if we can.

Time exists not only physically, but psychologically, Physically, there is time to learn a language, time to go somewhere, time by the watch, time by the sun's rising and setting, the darkness of night and the light of day. To put together a computer needs time. So time is necessary in a certain area.

Now we are questioning whether time exists at all psychologically, inwardly. Don't get depressed by all this; just look at it. The word *hope* implies time: I hope to be; I hope to become; I hope to achieve; I hope to fulfill; I hope to reach heaven, enlightenment. All that psychologically demands time. We are saying time in one area is necessary, but psychological time may be a total illusion. The etymological root of *illusion* is *ludere*, to play; to play with something. We play with illusions because that is fun. We take great pleasure in having a dozen illusions, the more neurotic they are, the better.

Is there tomorrow psychologically? Look at it, don't deny it. Don't get upset about it. Don't throw up your hands and say, "Buzz off." Look at it, watch it. Don't deny it or accept it. You might deny it because you are conditioned. Being conditioned, you might say, "I can't live with the idea of not having hope." That involves conditioning. Is it possible not to be conditioned? All these questions are interrelated.

What does *conditioned* mean? To be limited. Our brains are conditioned. If you understand this, if you are free of your conditioning, you will be an extraordinary person. It is not that you will be unconditioned because you are extraordinary, but understand it first, then naturally it happens. There are many scholars and scientists and others who say the human brain, human beings, will always be conditioned by their language, by their food, by their clothes, environment, society, and so on. They say that you can modify that conditioning, but you can never be free from it. Great writers have written about it. We have discussed with prominent people who are convinced that human beings cannot be free from all conditioning.

Is it possible not to be conditioned? What is the factor of being conditioned? What causes the brain to be conditioned?

First of all, it *is* conditioned. There is the demand for security—we are not advocating insecurity, just listen to the whole story of it. We want security physically, which is natural: to want food, clothes, and shelter is natural. Everybody in the world must have it, not just the few. Security is denied when it is only for the few; when there is poverty, there must be conflict. The essence of the brain is thinking. It is the nature of the brain to think. But thinking has realized that it is in itself uncertain, therefore it seeks security. And that security is sought through division: "I am an American," "my family," "your family."

Is there a security that is not of time, that is not of hope? Is there a security that is not put together by desire? Look at it very carefully. We need security; physical security, and that is being denied by all the religious, political, racial, ideological divisions, wars, in the world. Physical security is gradually being eroded. The desire to find security inwardly as separate human beings is causing that.

Find out if there is security inwardly. There is no security in attachment, whether it is attachment to my wife, to my friend, to my girl, to my man, or to an idea, to a concept, to an image. There is no security in those. Before you had not examined this, you were just attached. But now, by examining it, there has been a radical change. The brain has been conditioned by attachment. In that attachment to a wife or husband, to a job, to an ideal, to some god, it sought security.

So, when it discovers that there is no security in any of that, what has happened to the brain? What has happened to your brain? Traditionally, it has been conditioned to be attached, hoping to find security; and suddenly it discovers there is no security. What has happened to the brain? There has been a total change. You clung to a particular comforting attachment, and in that attachment you sought security. You find now, after very careful observation, that there is no security in that. You have moved away from it, so your brain is unconditioned. That unconditioning has been brought about because you saw the truth that in attachment there is no security. The seeing that there is no security in illusion is intelligence. That intelligence, the beginning of that, gives you absolute security in intelligence, not in attachment. It is very interesting, all this, if you go into it; more fascinating than any cinema in the world. You take a long journey, a journey that is endless, infinite. It implies that where there is intelligence, there is compassion.

Now let's go back to fear. Is there an ending to it? Not for one day, or a few hours, but the total ending of it? I realize what fear does. It darkens my whole life; it cripples my thinking; it's a physical shrinking, a nervous tension. I know very well what fear is. I know several forms of fear; but I am not concerned about the forms of fear, because if I can root out the cause, then I don't have to bother with the branches of it. I am not concerned with trimming the tree of fear, I am concerned with the ending of fear. Is that possible? Or must we everlastingly live with fear? Man has lived with fear for thousands of years, and you come along and say one can end it. What right have you to say it? Is it just another verbal fiction, or is it a fact?"

We will go into it together. You must see it for yourself, not I see it and I tell you, and then you reject or accept. Together let's take the journey to find out whether it is possible to end fear totally psychologically. Then outwardly that will have its own expression: when, psychologically, there is an ending of fear, then the ending has its own expression outwardly. Not the other way round. Time is a factor of fear. That is a fact. And also thought is a factor of fear: I think tomorrow may be dangerous; I think I am going to be ill; I think of what the public might say; I have a job but I might become unemployed.

So time and thought are the root of fear. Go into it slowly. We explained the nature of time. Time is hope; time is becoming. There is time outwardly and inwardly. We see time is a factor of fear. Obviously; that is clear. And also thought is a factor of fear: I am here; thought says, "I might die." Thought is experience, knowledge. From experience, knowledge is stored in the brain as memory. Memory is the reaction to thought. And thought is always limited, because knowledge is always limited; experience is always limited. In the scientific world, in the biological world, however much knowledge they have, they have to have more and more. So knowledge now or in the past or in the future will always be limited. This is a

46

fact. Whatever thought does, its action is limited. So time and thought are the root of fear.

How am I to stop thought? Don't ever ask anybody "how." But observe! Look very carefully. Time and thought are the root of fear. It is not how to stop thought or time, but to see the fact that thought is the originator of fear. Realize that, see it. But you need time or thought to go from here to there. You are sitting there, and you have to go somewhere else; that requires time and thought. Otherwise you could not move. But psychologically, time and thought have bred fear. And you are fear; you are not separate from fear. So the examiner of fear is the examined. The examiner who says time and thought are the root of fear, after looking at it carefully, sees that he is time and thought. You are the trap of fear. Get it? You are fear.

This is a revelation. Before, you said, "I am afraid; I will do something about it. I will run away from it; I will become courageous; I will be this, I will be that." Therefore there is conflict in that. Whereas now you see for yourself that you are time and thought. So you cannot do a thing about it. I wonder if you realize this.

Do you realize the immensity of that statement, the depth of it—that you are that, and therefore you cannot possibly do a thing about it? Which means what? All action with regard to fear has ended. See what happens then. Before, you acted upon it; now you are not acting, you are no longer the actor. You are that; you are both the actor and the act. What takes place when you are that?

This is part of meditation. Look at it very carefully. Take it in your hands like a precious jewel, and look at it. You are that when all movement stops. When you realize you are that, all movements naturally stop. Movement is a waste of energy. Therefore, when there is no movement, you have that tremendous energy to look. And therefore there is the ending of it.

We have taken a long journey together through valleys and mountains and meadows and groves. We have understood a great deal. We have not learned. We have learned nothing, but we have observed. That observance has brought great light, great intelligence. And that intelligence operates. It is not "me" operating.

5

The Narrow Circle of the Self

WHY HAS THE BRAIN, which has evolved for millennia upon millennia, and had tremendous experience of every kind—sorrow, pleasure, and the uncertainty of death—not solved the problem that there is no peace on earth? Who is going to solve the problem? The leaders? New leaders? New political statesmen? New priests? A new ideology? We have tried all that. Mankind has tried every way to bring about peace in the world and also peace in ourselves. And the brain, which is a very, very complex affair, capable of extraordinary technological progress, has not solved its problems.

Is the function of the brain just to go on living like this, acquiring great knowledge in every field and using that knowledge to destroy each other, to destroy the earth, nature? We all see this happening. Most of us are concerned only with ourselves, if we are at all frank and honest. There is self-interest in the most highly qualified people, intellectuals, and so on, and in the most primitive people, in the educated and the uneducated. The sophisticated and the religious people may identify themselves with something noble, but that very identification is part of self-interest. The brain, our brain, is concerned mainly with personal problems. There are problems of mathematics, problems of computers, and so on, but basically we are concerned with ourselves. That is a fact. However much we may try to hide the self-interest in noble work, in meditation, in belonging to various groups, self-interest dominates, consciously or unconsciously. If we are honest, look into ourselves and our political and religious activities, we see that we are concerned basically with ourselves. We have lived that way from the beginning of time, and we are still living that way. So the brain functions only in a very small, limited field.

Is the whole function of the brain to be concerned with itself, with its problems, with its pleasures and sorrows and pain, ambition, greed? That is the way we have lived; and the result of that in the world is chaos, each one wanting to fulfill, wanting to achieve—whether it is illumination, enlightenment, or becoming a big businessman, it is the same thing. So we have reduced our brain, which is an extraordinary instrument, to something petty. We have reduced that brain to be very limited. It may be extraordinarily capable in the technological world; there are marvelous instruments of war, instruments of surgery, medicine, communication, computers. There, the brain has functioned with an extraordinary vitality, with extraordinary capacity. Yet that very brain is concerned mainly with its own self-protective activity. This is all obvious fact.

The brain lives on memories and not on facts. This is very important to understand if we are going to explore what quality of a brain can penetrate and find out its deep function. We are dealing with facts only, which is that we are a series of movements of memory. Memory has become extraordinarily important, but it has nothing to do with facts. My son is dead; he is gone, and I remember. There is only remembrance. I live on the memories of those incidents we had together. I cherish those memories. Please, you are doing this, I am not telling you something that you are not doing. We are a series of movements of memory and time. Memory is time. Memory is the reaction of experience, knowledge, and the things that one has remembered. This is what the self is, what we are.

I do not know if you have ever inquired into what the present is, what "now" is. Is it the cessation of memory? Or do we not know what the "now" is at all? May I go into it a little bit? Mathematically, zero contains all the numbers. Zero was invented by the ancient Hindus, and in the zero all the numbers are contained. Is the "now" the totality of all time?

You see, the brain, having cultivated self-interest, which is the accumulation of memories, has become a very small psychological instrument. Obviously. When I am thinking about myself all day long, it is a very small affair. Or when I think about the whole world, it is still a small affair. Why has the brain got caught in this narrow circle of the self? The self, the "me," the ego, is nothing but words and memories. It is so. And that self has become so terribly important. When one is concerned with oneself, all one's actions must be psychologically limited. And where there is limitation there must be conflict. I am a Jew, you are an Arab; that is a limitation, a tribalism that is limited. And I cling to my limitation, and you cling to your limitation, and therefore there is perpetual conflict. If you are constantly repeating, "I am Russian," and you identify with that particular country, tradition, language, and all the literature of that country, it is very limited.

The brain, seeking security in the self, has made itself limited psychologically. So there is a contradiction between the psychological limitation and the extraordinary limitless technological progress. Is the function of the brain to live perpetually in conflict, and therefore never to have liberation, freedom? Is it the function of the brain just to be limited, to live in a small area psychologically? When one understands the nature of the self, is it possible to break down this limitation? And who is to break it down? This limitation has been brought about by thought, which has created or sought security in the limitation. And thought itself is limited. Thought is the outcome of vast experience, accumulated knowledge stored in the brain, in the very brain cells. One is not a brain expert, but has watched very carefully. Thought is the outcome of memory. As memory is limited, knowledge will always be limited, and experience is never complete.

The brain is functioning with the only instrument, the limited thought, so we are perpetually living in conflict, in struggle, in pain and sorrow, because we seek security in the limitation, in memories. That is simple. It is the function of the brain to find security for physical survival. One must survive physically, but one seeks physical security and also psychological security. Is there psychological security at all? Have we reduced our life just to seeking self-security in limitation? Physically there is no security, because of wars, racial or tribal conflict, ideological conflict. Is the only function of the brain to seek security in limitation? That is what we are doing, and in the search for security in limitation we are bringing about havoc in the world, great disorder, confusion. Again, that is obvious.

Now, what is the function of thought? That is the only instrument the brain has. What is thought? What is thinking? We all think, whether we are highly educated, sophisticated, or the most uneducated person, hungry, with very little food. So thinking is common to all of us. It is not *your* thinking. You may think and express it differently. You may be an artist, you may be a mathematician, biologist, and so on, and I may be a layman, but we both think. So thinking is not yours. Thinking is not individual. Please, this is a fundamental thing to understand. And yet this is what we are doing. We have reduced the whole vast process of thinking to "mine": "This is what I think"; "My opinion, my judgment, my values." See what is happening to us.

The brain has evolved through time, through thousands

upon thousands of years of experience, knowledge. There are all the activities of thought in the world, technological, personal, and so on. And we say, "It is my brain through which I think." Is that so? Is your brain yours? Or is it the result of thousands of years of evolution? It is not your brain, or my brain. It is brain. I wonder if you see the depth of this.

The brain is the center of our consciousness. What is your consciousness? Not according to the experts, but when you ask yourself that question, what is your consciousness? It is your beliefs, your conclusions, your opinions, your two thousand years of being programmed as a Christian, or five thousand years as a Hindu. Your consciousness is the reactions, the reflexes, the fears, the pleasures, the sorrows, the pain, the grief, and all the misery of human beings. That is your consciousness. Is your consciousness different from another's? Or is your consciousness like the consciousness of all humanity? People also suffer in Russia, in India, in China. They may have different garments, the environment may be different, but psychologically the content of our consciousness is common; it is shared by all human beings. Your brain and your consciousness are shared by all human beings, so you are the rest of mankind. You may be German, Swiss, a proud Englishman, but you are the rest of mankind. This is not an intellectual concept; it is not an idea, something romantic or sentimental. It is a fact! When that is deeply real, when that is the truth, then your whole outlook on life changes. Then you are responsible for all humanity. It is rather frightening, but it is so.

In our investigation we are not being self-centered, we are not cultivating the self more and more. We are not making the self more intelligent. We are like the rest of mankind. Out of that comes compassion.

Is the brain an instrument that is concerned merely with psychological and physical security? If it is not, then what is the function of the brain? If I am not concerned with myself everlastingly, even in my meditation—you know all that kind of silly stuff—then what place has thought? And is there a new instrument altogether that is not the activity of thought? We can see what thought has done in the technological world and the human world. Thought has built the most extraordinarily beautiful things: architecture, paintings, marvelous poems, great novels. But also thought has divided people, and through division it has created wars. Therefore thought is not the instrument of peace. Thought, being in itself divisive, limited, cannot possibly bring about peace in the world. It is shown: the League of Nations, the United Nations; Napoleon tried to conquer, unify, Europe; so did poor Hitler. The activity of thought cannot possibly resolve human problems. If you see that very clearly, then what?

Suppose I see very clearly what thought has done in the world, and I see very clearly what thought has done in the realm of my own psyche. The search for security is the basis of the movement of thought; but is there security at all through thought? Or is there security only when thought, with its own intelligence, with its own cunningness, realizes its place and does not enter into the area of the psyche?

We cannot live by ourselves. Life is a movement in relationship. In that relationship there are innumerable problems: sexual, psychological, of companionship, loneliness, the whole problem of relationship. So what is relationship? When you are related to your wife or to your father, husband, what is it? When you say, "I am related," what does that word mean? Not the dictionary meaning of it, which we all know, but what is the depth of it, the significance of that word? I am related to my wife, and in this relationship there is perpetual conflict. When we ask about relationship, we are trying to find out if this conflict can end. End! So to find out whether it can end we must face the actual fact of what our relationship is to another, however intimate it may be.

Is our relationship based on thought? You have to answer to yourself. Two friends are talking things over together. One asks the other why there is conflict in relationship. Is relationship based on thought, on memory, on pleasant or unpleasant incidents that have passed, that have happened? There is the memory of those, and each one of us lives on those memories, which is thought. I am ambitious and my wife is ambitious. She wants to fulfill in her way, and I want to fulfill in my way. She has come to some definite conclusions, and so have I. So there is always this division. And where there is division there must be conflict. This is simple.

So to understand the nature of conflict, and to see whether it is possible to end conflict in relationship, we have to ask whether thought dominates relationship. Then, is thought love? Go into it. It is thought in relationship that has bound us together through memory, through reactions, through pleasure, sexual and otherwise. And thought is the factor in relationship. She has said something to me that has hurt me; and I have hurt her. That hurt is being carried on, which is memory. It is like two parallel lines never meeting. And this we call relationship. Whether it is to your guru, whether it is to a woman or man, whether it is relationship to your political leader or to the priest, it is all based on thought and memory.

Is remembrance the activity of love? Please ask this question. If it is, we are living on dead memories. Memories are not in the future. Memories are the past. Is there a way of living in relationship in which memory doesn't enter? One may ask these questions, but merely asking questions is not the solution of the problem. Is it possible to live with another without the accumulation of memory about the other? Which is the ending of thought. So, is love the activity of thought?

As we are trying to find out how to live in this world peacefully, we have to understand the depth and the nature of thought and memory. Most of us from the beginning of our childhood till now bear the burden of many hurts, many psychological wounds, and the memory of those wounds, and the continuation of those hurts. Can all that be wiped away? If I am hurt, how can I love another? This is real inquiry so that you begin to see for yourself directly that there is a possibility of ending conflict. And the truth of that possibility exists only when you have really deeply inquired into the whole nature of the self and self-interest, which is based on reward and punishment. Then you begin to find out for yourself that thought is not the instrument in the solution of human problems. Even with technological problems, you may think a great deal to work them out, but you come to a state there too when thought is in abeyance—and you discover something new. If you merely continue in the field of knowledge all the time, there is nothing new.

We are inquiring into whether the brain can live in peace and therefore affect society. And it may not; we are not seeking an effect. If each one of us sees the truth of the activity of thought, the limitation of thought, and all the activities of memory and the division and consequent conflict, and lives in another way, what effect will this have on the vast public? None! Does it matter? Are you concerned with changing society, making it more orderly? You really are not, actually, if you face the fact. Therefore, if one may point out, it is a wrong question to ask what effect it will have on society if there is a fundamental mutation in *your* brain. Through facts you are seeking truth! That truth will act! *You* will not act.

What is intelligence? How do you receive that question? How do you approach that question? Our brain is trained to solve problems. It is trained from childhood to solve problems: mathematics history, examinations, architectural problems, engineering problems, problems of how to put a motor together. We approach life with a brain that is trying to solve problems. We treat life as a problem, and then try to find a solution to the problem. So when you are asked what intelligence is, you make that into a problem. Naturally. And then you try to solve that question through a brain that is trained to solve problems.

Now can one look at the question of what intelligence is—and not as a problem? Can you do it? If you do, that is the beginning of intelligence. That means the brain is already becoming free from its conditioning. But if you approach this as a question, and then try to solve it, you are back in the old muddle. When one realizes that the brain is conditioned to solve problems and therefore that you approach any question with a mind, with a brain, that says, "I must solve it," you never meet a challenge afresh. To meet a problem, any problem, afresh, is the beginning of intelligence.

Whether you like it or not, you are the rest of humanity. You may stick to your conditioning that you are an individual, but you are not. You may have a different body, different name, be a different color; you may have long hair, short hair; you may speak German, or Russian; but you are standing on the same ground as the rest of humanity.

We said that the brain has its function, and asked what the root of that function, the basis of that function, is. It is not to live in conflict, obviously. That question is raised, and you say, "Now I must solve it." Then you ask, "How am I to do it?" Then you get the systems, the methods, the apologies, and all the rest of it, the arguments, the pros and cons. But when the brain is not approaching a challenge, an issue, with its old trained conditioning, then you can look at that question, that challenge, totally anew, freshly.

Isn't it the capacity of intelligence to look at something clearly, not to try to solve it?

6

Can the Brain Be Totally Free?

T HE ACT OF LISTENING is very important if we are going to explore, to think together, into the whole problem
of our present-day existence. One must listen very carefully,
not only to what is being said but also to our own reactions to
what is being said, our reactions of approval or disapproval,
our sense of restrictions, our resistances, our fears, and all the
complexities of our reactions to any form of stimulation.

We are very circumscribed, limited, so limited that most
of us are unaware of it. Our brains have been so programmed
and conditioned. We are conditioned, shaped, molded by the
environment, by tradition, by religion, by the solitude of our
own illusions, our own imaginations, the solitude of our own
aspirations. Having listened to a great many people talk about
the brain, specialists and others, one perceives that through the
long process of evolution our brains are very limited. Apparently only a very small part of it acts or thinks or lives, the rest
is in abeyance. We can see for ourselves without relying on experts that our life is very small. We are so concerned with ourselves, with our success, with our miseries, and all the turmoil
of our own limited life, the sorrow, the pain, the anxiety, the

various forms of reaction that arise from our prejudices, our biases, our tendencies. All this does condition our brain, and so we never have the awareness of the whole of life, the whole of existence that is vast, immeasurable and tremendously potent.

Inquiry by itself has very little meaning. Inquiring into ourselves, into our environment, into the state of the world merely intellectually or out of curiosity, to acquire information, has very little effect on our lives; it is a waste of time and energy. But could we inquire easily and happily into ourselves, into the quality of our own life, into the nature of our behavior, into the whole process of our thought, into the way of our thinking, why we think the way we do, why human beings who have lived on this beautiful earth for so many millennia are still what they are, unhappy, violent, ready to kill each other for some idiotic reasons?

Could we look at this whole world in which we live, the world that we have created? This society is the result of our own complex life. You are conditioned by health, by environment, by culture, by nationalism, and so on. Unless we break through all this conditioning, we will go on as we have been going on for thousands of years. Violence will go on, corruption, each one isolated, seeking his own fulfillment and pursuing his own ambitions. And where there is isolation there must be conflict! It is no good merely talking about ideas, expressions, reactions, but can we go into this with tremendous energy, vitality, and see if it is possible to break down this conditioning so that the brain will have immense capacity?

The brain has extraordinary capacity now in the technological world, in computers, biological chemistry, genetic engineering. And various forms of other activities from the outside affect the brain. From the outside, scientists in the various disciplines are trying desperately to bring about a change in human beings. They are trying through genetic engineering to change the very genes themselves so that the human being is something entirely different. And the computer is taking over a great deal of our activity.

Communists have tried through authority, through discipline, through demanding complete obedience, to change the environment, hoping that would change human beings. They have not succeeded. On the contrary, they are creating great misery in the world. We are asking whether it is possible not to be affected from the outside. The "outside," whether it is "God," music, art, or the external laws that are established by governments, the outside agencies in various forms and disciplines are trying to force people to conform, to bring about a radical change in their behavior so that they will live without wars. They are also preparing for wars. Every government throughout the world is armed, ready to kill and be killed. This is going on all the time around us. I am sure most of us are aware of all this.

Religions have tried to change human beings, to tame us through fear, heaven and hell, and so on; and they have not succeeded either. These are all facts, not imagination or bias. This is what is going on in the world around us, affecting mankind through propaganda, through various forms of chemical engineering. These have never succeeded, and they will never succeed, because the psyche is far too strong, far too cunning, extraordinarily capable. Since all outside influences, including the idea of "God" and ideologies, various forms of historical dialectical conclusions, have not changed mankind, is it possible for human beings to change radically, fundamentally, without external influence at all? What it is essential to ask is whether each one of us is capable of bringing about a fundamental, deep mutation in the very brain cells themselves.

What will bring about a mutation in the brain cells themselves, not from the outside, not through genetic engineering, bio-chemistry, and so on? What will change the brain cells them-selves, which have been conditioned for thousands of years? I hope you are putting this question to yourself. If you are serious and earnest and passionate enough to put this question, what would be your answer? If you have thought a great deal about all this, you would say either that it is not possible, and so close the door to your further inquiry, or you would say, "I really don't know." We are in that position. We are not closing the door by saying it is impossible. How can mankind's brain, which has been conditioned for thousands and thousands of years through vast knowledge, experience, transform itself? Can the brain, which has such extraordinary capacity in one direction, and which is so utterly limited, circumscribed, conditioned, programmed, be totally free?

Not free to do what we like. We are all doing that anyhow, pursuing our own pleasures, our own solitary ambitions, our own salvation if you are at all religiously minded, our own isolated pleasures and illusions. We do that every day of our life. That is a common occurrence for all of humanity, pursuing our own isolated, solitary illusions, stimulations, aspirations, and ideologies. And that is what we call freedom. Surely, that is not freedom. Freedom requires a great deal of discipline. Freedom implies great humility, innate, inward discipline and work.

Most of us are arrogant because we rely so much on our knowledge. We are certain; our beliefs, our conclusions, our desires are so strong that we have lost all sense of deep, natural humility. How strong it is when someone says, "I am a Frenchman," or "I am British"! When you identify yourself with a country, with certain ideologies, with conclusions, concepts, then you are incapable of being humble. It is only when you inquire in humility that you learn, you find out. Then you see things as they are around you and in yourself.

Discipline is constantly watching—watching your own reactions, continual observation, seeing what the source of your thought is, why you react in certain ways, what your biases are, your prejudices, your hurts, and so on. Constant watching brings its own natural discipline, order. That is what we mean by discipline; not conformity, not following a certain pattern established by society or by yourself, but the eternal watching of the world and of yourself. Then you see there is no difference between the world and yourself. That brings about naturally a sense of order. Therefore order is discipline, not the other way round.

Work is not only physical work, which unfortunately most of us have to do, but work is also the sense of applying what you see to be true, applying it without having a period of time between perception and action. When the speaker saw many years ago as a boy that nationalism is a poison, he was no longer a Hindu; he just walked away. He was no longer a Hindu; he was finished with all those superstitions. You know all that rubbish that goes on in every nationality. I hope you don't mind my saying all this.

So, to live on this earth peacefully, in spite of the governments, requires a great deal of inquiry. To live peacefully demands great intelligence. Merely listening to what is being said seems so futile; but if, at the moment you see something to be true, there is instant application, then that removes conflict all together. Conflict exists only when there is a gap, a division between what you see to be actual, to be true, and your action. If there is an interval, a gap, a hiatus, that brings about conflict.

We are not doing any kind of propaganda. We are not trying to convince you of anything. On the contrary, one must have doubt, skepticism, and question, not only what is being said, but one's own life, one's own beliefs. If you begin to doubt, it gives a certain clarity. It doesn't give you a feeling of great importance about yourself. Doubt is necessary in our exploration, in our inquiry into this whole problem of existence. Is it possible for human beings, who are perhaps somewhat neurotic, to wipe that away, and become sane, rational, and in-quire with such a brain? We are asking whether the brain cells can, without any influence from outside—from government, environment, religions, and so on—bring about a mutation in themselves. This is a serious problem that cannot be answered by yes or no, affirmative or negative. One must look at this question as a whole, not as British, French, or with some kind of religious, superstitious nonsense, or according to one's own particular discipline or profession. One must look at the whole of life as one unitary movement. If we do, then we can begin to ask if it is possible.

If we do ask that question, then what difference does it make if a few of us perhaps bring about a mutation? What effect has it on the world? That is the usual question. Right? I may change and you may change, a few of us may bring about a mutation; but what effect has that on the mass of people, on the governments? Will they stop wars, and so on? I think to ask what effect it has on others is a wrong question, because then you are not doing the thing for itself, but for how it will affect others. After all, beauty has no cause. To do something for itself, for the love of itself, may have an extraordinary effect. For example, we have talked for the last sixty years, unfortu-nately or fortunately. One might ask, "How has it affected the world? You go to various parts of the world, has it changed anybody at all?" I think that is rather a foolish question. We might ask, "Why does a flower bloom? Why is there a solitary star in the heavens in the evening?" The man who has freed himself from his conditioning never asks that question. In that there is compassion, with its great intelligence.

Do we realize that we are conditioned? Am I aware without any choice that my brain is conditioned? Or do I accept what another says and therefore say, "My brain is conditioned"? Do you see the difference? If I am aware that my brain is condi-tioned, that has a totally different quality. But if you tell me that I am conditioned, and then I realize that I am conditioned, it becomes very superficial. So are we aware that we are conditioned by our experiences? We are not saying that it is right or wrong; we are going to find out. We are conditioned by our culture, by our tradition, by our environment, by all the religious propaganda. Are we aware? If you are aware, then you ask, why?

Why is the brain conditioned? What is the nature of conditioning? Is it essentially experience and knowledge? Please go slowly with this. Experience conditions the brain. Obviously. And experience means knowledge. To learn to drive a car you need experience. You get into a car, drive it, and gather through that experience knowledge of how to drive a car. Is knowledge the basic factor of our conditioning? Knowledge is the repetition of a certain tradition. Knowledge is necessary; otherwise you couldn't move, you couldn't drive a car, you couldn't do a job, if you have a job. So in one area physical knowledge is necessary. But knowledge also conditions our brain. We are being programmed by newspapers, by magazines, by constant repetition that we are British or French or Indian. With this constant repetition, the brain becomes dull, repetitive, mechanical. And perhaps that seems a safe way of living, but it has tremendous danger. The repetition of various countries' cultures is an isolating process, and therefore there is division, war. That is only one of the reasons for war. So are we aware that our brain is being programmed?

Please look at yourself. If one is aware that one is programmed, conditioned, then one asks if it is by knowledge. And apparently it is knowledge. Then why is the structure of the psyche essentially based on knowledge? The psyche, the "me," the self, is essentially a movement in knowledge, a series of memories of knowledge. We are a series of memories; so we *are* memory. Do you see that fact? It is not that we are divine and all that blah that is trotted out by religion. The actual fact is that we are nothing but memories. Most unpleasant discovery, isn't it? Or do you say, "Look, there is part of me that is not memory"? The moment that you say that, it is already memory. When I say I am not wholly the result of memories, that very statement implies that there is part of me which is not. But when I look at that part, it is also memory. Memories are the past modified by the present and may be projected into the future, but it is still a series of memories.

Please let's not become sentimental or romantic about all this; that is so meaningless. These are facts. What are you without memory, without all the remembrances of your achievements, of your wife, of your son, of your brother, family, memories of your travels, what you have done? They are all in the past. So memories are dead things. On those dead things we live. Do see all this.

Then the question arises: is it possible to live psychologically without a single memory? Put this question, please, to yourself. My brother, son, wife, husband, is dead. I remember all the incidents, happiness, intimate relationships. It is a vast reminiscence of the past, memory. And I live on that. I have a picture, photograph, and there is constant stimulation from the photograph. So the "me," the self, the ego, is a movement of identification with memory: "I am a Christian," "I am a Hindu," a Buddhist, an American, and so on. How tremendously attached we are to our identifications. That is our conditioning. And when you see that, not verbally, not as an idea, but actually see the fact, then there is action. Like when you have a violent toothache, there is action because it is there. But if you imagine you have a toothache, then that's quite a different process.

So do we see clearly for ourselves, without being persuaded, without being pushed into a corner, what we are, which is our conditioning, which is our consciousness? Seeing that, what is one to do? Have we reached that point when we realize completely that we are conditioned and that conditioning is a vast series of movements of memories? Memories are always the past, remembrance of things past that are then projected into the future, modified by the present. It is a movement of memories, and these memories we call knowledge.

Then how does one look at these memories? How does one observe these memories? We have thousands of memories. From childhood we have gathered pleasant, unpleasant memories of our aspirations, memories of achievements, memories of pain, fear, great sorrow. These are all memories. Do we see these memories as different from the observer? We are observing. I am observing that I am a long series of memories. I have stated that I am memories. But there is in me the feeling that I am not *all* that, that there is something else that is observing. So is the observer different from the observed? When you look at this, something extraordinary happens. It is not something mysterious, not parapsychological, and so on, it is something that ends conflict. And *that* is far more important than anything else.

As long as there is division between the memories and the observer, this division creates conflict. Between the Arab and the Jew, between the Briton and the Argentinean, between the Hindu and the Muslim: wherever there is division there must be conflict. Pursue that please. Wherever there is isolated action, isolated solitary pleasure, solitary aspiration, that very solitude is an act of separation. Therefore, that very person who pursues his particular ambition, his particular fulfillment, his aspirations, and so on, must inevitably create conflict, not only for himself but for others.

So from this arises the question whether conflict of every kind, in our very being, can end? Because we live with conflict. You might say, "Well, all nature is in conflict. A single tree in a forest is fighting to achieve light, is struggling, fighting, squeezing out others. And human beings, born from nature, are doing the same thing." If you accept that, then you accept all the consequences of conflict: wars, confusion, brutality, ugliness, the nastiness of war. As long as you are British, French, or Indian you are inevitably going to create wars. You see this, and don't do anything about it.

So, to end conflict, which means to live with that peace which requires tremendous intelligence, understand the nature of conflict.

7

Consciousness Is Shared by All Human Beings

P EACE CAN EXIST only if we have complete security outwardly and inwardly, environmentally and psychologically. We all want security; every animal, every living thing needs security. Apparently we do not have security. We have sought it in following religions, beliefs, ideologies, in some form of authority, and yet we remain separate. Is it that each one seeking his or her own particular form of security—thinking they are separate, isolated entities—is one of the basic causes why human beings must inevitably come into conflict with others who are also seeking their own particular form of security? Are we separate from the rest of humanity? Are you a separate individual seeking your own happiness, your own pleasures, solitary in your illusions, in your particular form of imaginative hope? This is a question that must be gone into, because if that is the cause of it, either the cause is rational, real, actual, and then we have to deal with that, or it is really illusory. Each one of us has been brought up to think that we are individuals, separate. Is that a fact? Our consciousness contains our behavior, our reactions, our pleasures, fears, anxieties, sorrow, and all the experiences, knowledge. All that is our consciousness is what we are, what each one of us is. Is that consciousness different from the rest of humanity's?

When you observe the world, you see that all human beings go through more or less the same forms of suffering, anxiety, insecurity. They believe in some kind of illusory nonsense, are full of superstitions, fears. Everywhere human beings go through all this, being insecure, uncertain, fearful, constantly in conflict, burdened with great sorrow. This is a fact. So is your consciousness different from the rest of mankind's? I may be an Arab, with my particular Islamic tradition, and as a human being, apart from the label as an Arab, I go through all the turmoil of life, like you do—pain, sorrow, jealousy, hate. So is there a difference, apart from labels, apart from culture, between me, as an Arab, and you? Please consider all this.

One must be absolutely clear for oneself about this matter. It is your psyche, and the content of the psyche is its own consciousness. That consciousness is shared by all human beings. Though outwardly we may have a different culture, different environment, different food, different clothes, be more affluent, essentially, deeply, most profoundly we are the rest of the world, and the world is us. Be quite clear on this point. You may not like it, because we have been brought up from childhood, perhaps before childhood in the very genes, to think that we are separate individuals. We are questioning that very thing, not only subjectively but objectively.

If you examine without any bias, without any tradition, if your brain is eager to find out whether it is possible to live in this world with complete freedom and peace and therefore with order, you have to put this question. You may be a great scientist, a great painter, a marvelous poet, but the scientist, the poet, the painter have their own sorrow, pain, anxiety like the rest of us. And as long as we think we are separate, conflict must exist—between the Arab and the Jew, between the black and the white, between the Muslim and the rest of the world.

We must consider this question seriously, exercise our brains, not accept.

Is one of the causes of war, one of the causes of conflict between human beings, this fallacy that each one of us is entirely different? And if we are not different, then we are the rest of mankind. You *are* the rest of mankind. With that goes tremendous responsibility, which you may not like to have. We like to avoid responsibility. As long as you are violent, aggressive, you contribute that to the rest of the world's, to the rest of mankind's, aggression, violence. This is natural. If you are the rest of mankind—you are mankind, not part of mankind, you are the entire world—and you have that feeling, see the truth of that, then your outlook is entirely different. Then you have totally abolished all division. I wonder if you see the truth of this; not as sentimentality, not as a romantic, utopian concept, but as an actuality, a fact.

Let's examine it more closely. As long as there is separation between me and you, we and they, between man and woman, between you and your wife, the wife and the husband, the family and the community, the community and the larger community, conflict must exist in our relationships. We all know this. So why is there conflict in our relationships? One is married, with children, or unmarried, and in all human relationships conflict exists as long as the husband or the wife or the woman or the man is pursuing his or her own sense of fulfillment, both sexually and in the world. This is a fact, isn't it? The wife pursues her own particular form of pleasure, and the husband pursues his own, so actually they never meet, except perhaps in bed. That is a fact.

Now is it possible to be free of this separation? Then one begins to inquire into the nature of what is called affection, into the nature of what love is. If we are serious, as we must be considering what the world has become—insane, disorderly, corrupt, all the ugly things that are going on—looking at all this, we must inevitably ask why. In close relationship where there is a sense of affection, tolerance, acceptance, is there conflict, divorce, hate, the whole field of turmoil? Is it possible to live with another completely at peace? What do you say to all this? It is your life, and you have to answer these really serious questions, not evade them.

As long as we are caught in the illusion of individuality, however close our relationship with another, however intimate, however personal the companionship in the escape from loneliness, this question must be answered. Because all life is relationship—with nature, with the universe, and with the tiniest little flower in the field; and also in relationship with another human being. We cannot live without relationship. Even the monk who has taken various forms of vows is related. Yet, in our relationships, conflict seems to be all-pervasive. We must start very near to go very far to see whether we can live without conflict and therefore with peace. We must start where we are, with our families, with ourselves.

Looking at the world together, looking at our relationships together, as friends we can question each other, we can doubt what we are saying without hurting each other because we are friends. And out of this friendship, we can understand the depth and the beauty of relationship in which there is no conflict. Relationship is extraordinarily important. It is our life. And as long as there is conflict, relationship becomes most destructive.

How do you observe all this? How do you observe this conflict, the present state of the world, our present relationships with each other? It is very important to understand the nature and the structure of the observer. Do I observe the fact that we are separate, each with his own ambitions, his own greed, his own particular form of irritation? In my observation, I may be biased, prejudiced, so it is very important for me to find out the nature of the observer. If I am not clear how to observe, in what manner to look, I may distort the whole thing. So I must inquire into the nature of the observer. Unless a scientist is very clear both subjectively and objectively, so that he is observing without any bias, without any prejudice, without the self entering into his observation, his observation will be distorted, untrue, nonfactual. Similarly, we have to be very clear about the nature of observation and who the observer is.

If you ever look at trees, at a field full of cows or sheep, or see the horizon lit up by the morning sun—how do you observe all that? When you look at a tree or a house, your very perception is blocked by the word you use. I can look at a Frenchman and say, "Oh, he is a Frenchman." That means that all my prejudices, all my knowledge of the French, come in between me and observing someone who calls himself French. So can I look without all the prejudices, antagonisms? Can you?

The observer is the past. The observer is full of his past knowledge, and whether that knowledge is absurd, silly, or actual, that knowledge is blocking his observation. To observe my relationship with my wife or husband, I must observe without any previous, accumulated incidents, knowledge. Is that possible? Otherwise, I never see my wife for the first time; I am always looking at her with all the memories of a thousand days. A living thing can never be observed with limited knowledge. And knowledge is always limited. A living thing must be observed freely, without all the accumulation, experiences of knowledge. So is it possible for me to look at my wife or husband, or girlfriend or whatever you like, without the previous remembrances?

Have you ever tried to look at a tree without the word *tree*, to look at a flower without the label, so that you are actually observing what actually is, in which there is no subjective reaction?

You see, our brain is a network of words, a network of remembrances. It is never free to look because it has been conditioned through identification. To us, identity is very important.

If I am "Hindu," it gives me a sense of assurance, a sense of security. I have roots in that—like the British, like the French, the German, the rest of the world. Can I look, observe, without any identity? Are you doing it now? Or are you going to try to do it later? To do it now, the very action of perception is to destroy that division. If you do it *now*, it means action is not of time.

Look. I have heard this. I have paid attention to what I have heard. I am sitting next to my wife or husband. I am a serious person and I hope she or he is too. And I see that I am not looking freely, without any past incidents, and so on. And it is important to me to have a relationship with her, or with him, in which there is no conflict, because if I can live that way, I have peace in my heart and brain. So the very moment I hear this, there is the actual perception that I am in conflict and that I am looking at her, or him, with all the accumulated dead memories. So I am not looking at her or him. Action is the moment of perception of the fact, and not allowing time to interfere with the action. So, can I look at her, or him, without any past remembrances?

Will you do it now? See what it entails. Do it, and you will find out how tremendously we are bound to the past. Our life is past memories. Apparently they have a strong hold on our brain; and we say it is impossible to look without the knowledge of yesterday, so we give up and pursue the old way, quarreling, nagging, fighting, being miserable, unhappy. Can one actually see the fact that conflict must exist between two human beings, and therefore with the rest of humanity, as long as there is this concept of the "individual," with its own particular memories? Seeing that is to act, not postpone action. When you postpone action, time is involved; and during that postponement, other things take place; other complexities arise. So action is perception and instant action, so that your brain is not cluttered with problems.

Why do human beings have problems at all? Our brains, from childhood, are trained to solve problems. The poor child! At the age of two now, they are teaching babies to count, to learn a language. From childhood through school, college, university, business, family, everything has become a problem that must be solved. So we treat life as a vast problem, because our brain is trained that way. We never meet anything easily, happily; instead it becomes a dreadful problem to be solved. So relationship has become a problem. And when we try to solve a problem, in the solution of that problem, we have other problems from that very solution. That is what is happening politically. So can you look at life, not as a problem, though problems exist, and have a mind that is free from problems? See the difference? Problems exist. I have a toothache; I have to go to the dentist. Problems exist; but if my brain is free of problems, then I can deal with those problems easily. But if my brain is trained, conditioned to deal with problems, I increase problems.

There is a question, for example, about God. Whether God exists or not is a problem. Most Christians believe that there is God. Buddhists have no idea of God; he doesn't exist in their religious philosophy. But they make Buddha into a god; that is a different matter. Now, that is a problem. You believe and suppose I don't believe. Are you willing to look at why God exists, if he does exist? Can you look at that question and find out why, throughout the ages, man has invented God? I am using that word *invented* purposely. I hope you will not get hurt. Man has invented it because he is frightened. He wants somebody, an outside agency, to protect him, to give him security; he wants to feel that somebody out there is looking after him. That concept gives great comfort. Whether that is an illusion or an actuality doesn't matter. But as long as you have that kind of belief, it gives you great comfort. Now, if you strongly believe in all that, would you doubt it, question it, find out? Or are you so frightened, you won't even think about it?

To find out whether there is something beyond man's measure, one must be free to inquire. As we inquired into relationship, one must be free to inquire, to observe. And if the observer, the inquirer, is prejudiced, is convinced deeply, though he may pretend outwardly to examine, then his examination will be according to his conviction. So can the brain be free to look, to look at one's wife, husband, to look at all the governments, one's guru, the whole world around one, to look carefully without the background of tradition, values, judgments? The brain then is acting wholly, not in fragments.

Scientists say that only one very small part of the brain is functioning with most people and therefore their outlook on life is fragmentary. Only one part of my brain is actively sharing or actively operating throughout my life; and therefore the brain is not functioning wholly. Can the brain operate holistically, completely, not just a part? Are you serious enough to want to find out? The brain is now very limited because all knowledge is limited. You must be quite sure of that. All knowledge, whether it be the knowledge of the past or the knowledge of the future, is everlastingly limited. They are discovering more and more in the scientific world; no scientist can ever say his knowledge is complete. Knowledge is always incomplete. And knowledge being incomplete, thought is incomplete. Because thought is born out of knowledge as memory, thought is limited. Without memory you have no thought. Without knowledge there is no existence of thought. And we only function, now, with limited thought.

My thought and your thought, the thought of the great scientist or the uneducated individual, are similar. Thinking is similar. We may express it differently, but thought is limited. As long as our thinking is the basis of our action, the basis of our life, the brain can never function as a whole. Logically see this, please. Our lives are fragmented: "I am a businessman," "I am a scientist," "I am a painter," and so on, and so on. We are

all put in categories. Our life is fragmentary because our thinking is limited. Do you see the fact of it? You may be doubtful,
because we are cutting at the very root of our life, which is
thinking. Marvelous cathedrals, great architecture, great im-
plements of war, the computers, and so on, are all the product
of thought. And all the things in the cathedrals and the church
are the product of thought. Nobody can deny this. The vest-
ments, the robes that the priests put on, are copied from the
Egyptians. Thought has produced all this. And thought has
also invented God.

Now, the question is whether to eliminate thought altogether. And who is the entity who is going to eliminate all thought?
It is still thought. Your meditation, if any of you indulge in
that kind of stuff, is to eliminate thinking. But you never examine who is the eliminator, who is saying, "I mustn't think."
It is still thought that says, "By Jove, if I don't think I might get
something." And yet thought is necessary, knowledge is necessary in certain areas; otherwise you can't get home, you can't
write letters, you couldn't speak English, and so on.

So thought has been the instrument of our fragmentation.
Observe that; don't ask how to get rid of thought. Observe the
fact that thought is necessary in certain areas, and thought in
the psychological world may not be necessary at all. In our relationship with each other, if thought is the instrument, which
it is, then that very thought is the factor of divisiveness. See it;
don't ask what to do about it. See the danger of this; then you
move away from danger, as from a precipice, from a dangerous animal. Similarly, thought is dangerous in the psychological world. If you observe this very carefully, without any bias,
then thought begins to realize its own place.

8

Suffering and Death

I N TALKING OVER TOGETHER our human problems, not only the daily problems of our life but all the travail of existence, we should also go very much deeper in the inquiry into what is beyond all time. What is the source, the origin, of all creation? To enter into that area, one must begin, surely, with all the contents of our consciousness, with what we are: our reactions, our anxieties, loneliness, depression, elation, fears, the continuity of pleasure. And we must ask also if it is possible to end all sorrow, and inquire into what religion is, meditation, the nature of dying, and the whole limitation of time. We must go very deeply into these matters because always scratching on the surface as we generally do, we find very little. Could we go deeply into the whole question of whether the content of our consciousness can ever come to an end? That is, the ending of all our wounds, psychological hurts, fears, all the memories to which we cling and the pain, the pleasure, the great deal of grief and sorrow. All that makes up our consciousness, which is what we are.

Most of us are concerned with ourselves, with our own achievements, with our own successes, failures, and give ourselves great importance in doing little things. Can all that end

and can we discover something totally new? Not only discover, but experience. One must be very careful in using that
word *experience*. There is really nothing to experience. If you
go beyond time, if that is possible, and beyond fear and so on,
is there anything to experience? We are going to go into all
this together. You are not merely listening to a lot of words
put together into sentences and ideas; together we are going
to inquire and see if the programs with which our brains have
been so heavily conditioned can come to an end, and no longer
be programmed. If we are willing to give our interest, serious
intention, and considerable attention to it, perhaps we can see
if there is something infinite, beyond all time.

First of all, do we realize that thought is a material process
and therefore is limited? Any action based on that limitation
must inevitably create conflict. Thought is a material process.
Matter is limited energy; and the whole content of our consciousness is the result of the material process of thought. The content of our consciousness, with all the reactions and responses,
and so on, is put together by the material process of thought,
which is limited. So our consciousness, which is what we are,
is always limited.

When one is concerned with oneself, with one's problems,
with one's relationships, with one's status in society, and so on,
that concern with oneself is a very small affair, a limited affair. Do we actually see this or is it just an idea to be pursued,
inquired into, and then come to a conclusion, and accept that
conclusion and say, "I am that"? Or do we see immediately,
instantly, that all the self-centered activity is very, very limited.
Whether it be in the name of religion, in the name of peace, in
the name of leading a good life, and so on, this self-centered
activity is always limited and therefore the cause of conflict. Do
we actually realize that, or is it merely an idea?

Do we see the difference between the actuality and the
idea? If you pursue the idea, then you are following some kind

of illusion. So, do we actually realize that the self-centered, egotistic activity is very small and separate and, therefore, that the basic cause of conflict is the self? The self, the psyche, the persona is the whole content of our consciousness, which is our conditioning, which is our being programmed for millennia upon millennia, which is the whole structure of knowledge.

We are looking at the enormous, complex problems of existence of our daily life, which is generally rather shallow, monotonous, boring, or exciting, indulgent, pursuing various forms of pleasure, and—whether one has a jolly good life or a miserable life—ultimately ending in death. We try to give meaning to the shallowness, but that meaning, too, that significance, is still shallow. Realizing all this, could we together explore what we actually are, break down this limitation and, if possible, go further?

One of the factors in the content of our consciousness is fear. Most of us know what fear is, whether it is superficial or deeply embedded in the recesses of our brain. We are all afraid of something. Can that psychological fear end? Begin with that. Then we can ask whether there are physical fears also and about their relation to the psyche, to psychological fears. We are inquiring into the nature of fear, not the various forms of fear. One may be afraid of death, one may be afraid of one's wife or husband, one may be afraid of various things, but we are concerned with fear itself, the actual reaction that is called *fear*, not fear *of* something or fear of the past or the future.

What is the cause, the root of fear? Is it thought and is it time? Is it thought, thinking about the future or thinking about the past? And is time also the cause? Time is growing old, as most of us are; the moment we are born, we are already growing old. And time is future, not by the watch, by the day or by the year, but as a movement from what has been or what is to what should be, what might be. Is the whole movement of time, the psychological process of time, one of the causes of fear? The memory of some pain, both physical and psychological, which might have happened a couple of weeks ago, and being afraid that it might happen again, is the movement of time and thought. So are time and thought the causes of fear? Time is thought, because thought is the response of memory, which is knowledge and experience. Knowledge is of time, and knowledge may be one of the causes of fear.

We are saying that time, thought, knowledge, are not separate; it is an actual unitary movement that may be the cause of fear. It *is* the cause of fear. When one realizes that, even intellectually, verbally, is it possible to end that fear? What is your answer? If you are waiting for an answer, we are not working, thinking, investigating together. Our brains have been conditioned, trained, educated to learn from somebody else, be instructed by another. We have no authority to tell you what to do. Together see the whole movement of fear, what is involved in it, why human beings have borne this fear for thousands of years and have not solved it. They have transmitted it and accepted it as the norm of life, as a way of living.

In questioning whether fear can ever end psychologically, we must understand the cause of it. Where there is a cause, there is an end. If one has some kind of disease, and if after diagnosis you find the cause, it can be ended. Similarly, if we can find the cause, the basic cause, the fundamental cause of fear, then fear can end.

We are saying that time/thought, not two separate things, is the root of fear. Desire is also part of fear. Desire is thought with its image. Without an image, there is no desire. You see something, and thought creates the image of you having that. At that moment desire is born. So thought is essentially the movement of desire, and time/thought is the root of fear. How do I observe that fact? Suppose, I realize that thought/time with all its complexity is the root of fear. How do I realize it, feel it, be aware of it? Do I see time/thought as something separate from me, or am I that?

I am anger, am I not? Anger is not something separate from me. I am greed, envy, anxiety. I like to think they are something separate over which I have control, but the actual fact is I am all that. Even the controller is me. So there is no division between greed, anger, jealousy, and so on; that is me, that is the observer. So how does one observe this fact that time/thought is fear? How do you look at it—as something separate from you, or you are that? If you are that, and it is not separate from you, all action ceases, doesn't it? Before, you controlled, suppressed, tried to rationalize fear. Now you see that you are all that, and therefore the whole movement of time and thought stops.

We are all so eager to act. One *must* act, but here you have to watch the whole thing without any sense of doing something. Just observe without any reaction or response to what you observe.

We should also go into why humanity has suffered, and whether there is an ending to suffering, not only to the personal sorrow, but to the sorrow of vast humanity. Let's not get sentimental about this, but actually all of us suffer in one way or another. The dull person and the most intellectual, learned one suffer; every human being on earth, including the leaders, suffers. And we are asking whether that suffering can end.

Some of us enjoy suffering, which becomes neurotic. Let's not bother about the people who enjoy suffering, thinking that suffering in some way will help us to understand the universe, to understand life. One suffers. My son is dead, gone. But the memory remains, the memory of his companionship, of my affection, love for him, and so on. Memory remains. Is that memory sorrow? Please, inquire. I have lost my wife, or I am not as clever as you are; I am not as alert, sensitive as you are, and I suffer through that. Or I suffer in ten other different ways. Is suffering, the shedding of tears, over the actual loss; or does the loss bring about various memories, remembrances that are one of the causes of suffering, or are perhaps the major cause?

From our beginning, humans have had wars, have killed people. That has been our pattern of existence, war after war, killing thousands of people. Humanity has suffered; and we are still pursuing that path of war that has brought about tremendous sorrow for mankind. And we have our own personal sorrow. Sorrow is the same whether it is yours or mine. I like to identify myself with my sorrow, and you like to identify yourself with your sorrow. But your sorrow and my sorrow is the same. The objects of sorrow may vary, but sorrow is sorrow. Therefore it is not personal. It is very difficult to see the truth of this.

If you suffer, and I suffer, you suffer for one reason and I suffer for another, and we identify ourselves with our particular one. We divide ourselves and then find ways and means to suppress it, rationalize, and so on. But if we realize that sorrow is the sorrow of all humanity and that we are the rest of humanity because we have fears, sorrow, pleasure, anxiety like them, if we realize sorrow is not my sorrow, it becomes a small affair. We are the whole of humanity, and when there is suffering, that suffering is humanity's suffering. Then you have a totally different approach to the problem. If it is "my suffering," I pray, "Please, God, help me to get over it, to understand it"; and it all becomes so personal, a shoddy little affair. When it is the rest of mankind that has suffered, then suffering becomes an extraordinary thing that one has to look at very carefully. And if one human being understands the nature of suffering and goes beyond it, she then helps the rest of mankind.

Now, is suffering a remembrance? The mother or the father whose son has been killed in war remembers all the things that he did—the birth, the pictures, the photographs, all the incidents and accidents, and laughter, tears, scolding, and death. So, is sorrow part of this continuity of memory? And if it is memory, don't reduce memory just to a few words. It is a tremendous content. Can that memory, not only of my particular son, but also the memory of humanity's sorrow—that memory which is sorrow—can that memory come to an end?

One has to inquire not only into a particular memory, but into the whole movement of memory. We live on memories. We are memories. We are the word, the reaction to that word, the pleasure derived from the word, the remembrance of all the things that were. The symbol, the incident, accident, has been stored up in the brain and is awakened when an incident takes place. Memory is the past. So we are the past.

Can this whole movement of the past, which is time, which is thought, end? Not thought in our daily life, we are not talking of that. We are not talking about thought used to drive a car, to write a letter, to write a poem. There, thought, knowledge, is absolutely necessary. We are talking of this whole psychological movement, which is based on memory. We are asking a much deeper question, which is, can the self, the "me," the ego, all this self-centered activity that is the movement of memory, can that self end? Not by discipline, by control, by suppression or identification with something greater, which is still the movement of the self. Can that self end? You might then ask, if the self ends, what place is there for me in society? What shall I do? First end it, and then find out. Not the other way around.

This is a very, very serious question. Nobody in the world—or beyond the world—can tell you how to end it. I observe the fact that I am hurt psychologically because my daughter, my son, my father has done something that hurts me. Most people carry their hurt all through their life. If I can observe hurt without a single resistance, without any reaction that I should not be hurt or to hold on to it, just observe the hurt, the psychological wound, then I see that hurts disappear altogether. In the same way, just observe memory as it arises; see the nature of it, the evolution of it. The whole nature of activity of our daily life is based on this. And memory is very, very limited. Thought may invent the infinite, but thought being itself limited, its infinity is also limited, finite. But it may pretend that it is infinite.

All this implies complete freedom. Not only freedom *from* something, but the quality of freedom that is not based on any reaction, any reward or punishment. To inquire into that, one must also understand the nature of death, dying. One must inquire very quietly, not hysterically, into this very complex problem. Dying or coming to an end is what we are concerned about, talking about, because it is part of our life. It is not only that we are born, are educated, and go through all the troubles and anxieties, but death is also part of our life. It is there whether you like it or not; whether you are British or French, it is there. Whether you are young, middle-aged, or old, diseased, it is there. And one must understand what it is, as one must understand life before death. We have been trying to understand together what is before death, the fear, wounds, sorrow, pain, anxiety, labor, going to the office from morning till night. All that is part of our life, living, and so also is the ending of all that. One may have had a very good life, pleasant, successful, been somebody in the world, with power, position, money, but death is there at the end. We like to postpone it as long as possible, put it far away. The organism dies, naturally. It will live long if we treat it properly.

What is it to die? Not jump off a bridge, not do something to kill yourself, but living as we are now, sitting there, what is death? Apart from the brain lacking oxygen and the whole physical organism withering away, we are asking: is death an ending, an ending to everything that I have had—my wife, my children, my books, my status, my power, my position? You know all that is going to come to an end.

We must also inquire into the question of the East, which is about reincarnation—to be reborn, to have a series of lives till you reach whatever you reach, "the highest principle," and so on. They believe in that very strongly, but they don't deeply ask what it is that continues. Is it the "me" that is going to continue or is there something beyond the "me" that is going to continue? And if there is something beyond "me," my ideas, my opinions, my conclusions, and so on, if that "me" is the word, the name, the remembrances, is that going to continue? Or is there a spiritual entity—the soul in the Christian world, and the Buddhist world, the Hindu world have different words—that will continue? If that thing that is beyond "me" or that the "me" covers up, is a spiritual entity, it must be beyond time and beyond death. Therefore that cannot reincarnate. So people like to believe all that because it is a great comfort: "I shall be born next life. I've had a poor life, but next life I'll have a better house. In another life I'll live in a bigger house or I'll be a king," or some rot or other.

So, we put aside all that kind of illusory pursuit and face the fact that psychologically there is an ending, a complete ending. The "me," with all its memories, comes to an end. That is dying. And we don't like that, so we seek various forms of comfort, beliefs, faith, resurrection.

Now, while living, can we end something without any cause, without any future? End something. Take attachment, for example. Will you end all attachment: attachment to your name, attachment to your furniture, attachment to your wife, to your husband, to your garden, attachment to your ideas, prejudices? Will you end all attachments while living? That is what is going to happen when you actually die. So do it now and see what it means. That ending is tremendous, has a tremendous quality behind it. There is no attachment to anything. That is freedom, and when there is that kind of freedom, death has no fear, because you are already living with death. The two are going together, living and dying. Do you understand the beauty of that? The quality of complete freedom from all fear. Because, where there is attachment, there is jealousy, anxiety, hate. And the more you are attached, the more pain there is.

You know all this. If you went and told your wife or husband, "I am no longer attached to you," what would happen? Does it deny love? Does it deny relationship? Is attachment love? Inquire into all this, and the deeper you inquire, the more vitality and security and strength you have—and it isn't derived from any drugs, any stimulation.

9

In the Perception of What Is True, There Is Peace

Is IT POSSIBLE TO COMMUNICATE with each other deeply and go together for a long journey, a journey that covers the entire human status, not with the view of a particular country or a particular group of people or community, nor with any particular philosophy? If you are waiting to be instructed, informed, told what to do, I am afraid you will be disappointed. Together we are going to take a very long journey, not only outwardly in the physical world, but also in the psychological world, in the world that lies inside us, inside the skin, as it were; a world that few of us have taken seriously or have gone into very deeply. One must talk freely, intelligently, without any interpretation, without any conclusion, like two friends talking together not only about the world situation but also about their own problems, their own behavior, their own ways of thinking, their prejudices, opinions, conclusions. Listen not only to the network of words but also to the deeper issues of life.

Religion and to have peace in the world are the two most important things in life. The etymological meaning of the word *religion* is not very clear; but it is generally accepted to be what is going on in the world: the Christian religion, the Islamic, the Hindu, the Buddhist, and so on, with their temples and mosques and churches or cathedrals and all the rituals that go on and all the things inside them. Faiths, beliefs, the repetition of certain phrases, doing rituals, the whole structure of superstition is generally what is understood to be religion. That is not religion, it is all put together by thought. Thought is a material process that has created traditions and sanctified them. Then that very thought turns to worship that which it has created. This is a fact, not a theory.

We said there is no peace in the world. All nations prepare for war, including nuclear war and the destruction of the whole of humanity. There is no peace in the world, nor is there peace in ourselves. To be a religious human being and also to live peacefully in this world, without conflict, without problems, without this divisive process, requires a great deal of intelligence, not repetition of some slogans, not following some guru. All that is gone, finished in people who are at all aware and conscious of what is going on. Religion no longer has any meaning, except for sentimental, sensory excitement and emotional titillation. Religion in the deeper sense of that word refers to living a righteous life, a life of freedom, taking responsibility for one's own actions, independent of environment, and so on.

Let's be aware not only of the words and their significance but also of our own responses, our own interpretations, how we receive, accept, or react. We are going to take a long friendly, not dogmatic, journey, both outwardly and inwardly. It is far more difficult to take a journey inwardly. It is fairly easy to be well-informed of what is going on in the world, but one must have criteria to evaluate, to see things as they are in the outer world. It is really not an outward world at all; it is a world that we have created. It is like a tide, going out and coming in; it is the same water, but we have unfortunately divided the world as the outer and the inner.

It is an eternal movement of action and reaction, challenge and response, problem after problem. These problems are increasing, created not only by politicians but also by the religious people; and we have created problems for ourselves. We have created society; it hasn't suddenly come into being. This is what we are. If our house is burning, disorderly, competitive, ruthless, we have created such a society where there is brutality, cruelty, injustice, and so on. It is our responsibility not to change society but to see in our journey whether in the very movement of taking that journey there is the possibility of changing ourselves fundamentally, of a psychological revolution, not a physical revolution.

The world is divided geographically, nationally, by religion, by economics. The world is broken up, fragmented. That fragmentation has taken place through nationalism, which is glorified traditionalism. Each country is concerned with itself. But politicians and leaders forget that we are all human beings. *We are one people.* Though you may call yourself a Muslim, or a Hindu, or a Buddhist, or a Christian, we are one humanity. You may belong to a certain sect, assert your own personal ambitions, but behind all that we are one entity. The whole of humanity is us.

Unfortunately, for our own search for security through the family, through the community, through the nation, we have separated the world as American, Russian, French, Indian, Arab, Jew, and so on. This separation, this division, this fragmentation has been one of the causes of war, destroying each other in the name of God, in the name of religion, in the name of ideologies. We all know this. And this process, this division of tribalism, economics, religion, society, traditions, has been going on from the most ancient of times. Where there is division, fragmentation, there must be conflict, that is a fact. This is what is going on: one ideology going against another ideology, the conservative ideology against the liberal, the socialist against the communist, the fascist against everybody else. See what is taking place actually, daily in our life. Unless division ceases completely, so that one is no longer a Hindu, a Buddhist, a Muslim, a Christian or communist, socialist, capitalist, one is bound to create war, killing human beings by the thousands, by the millions. If nuclear war is to take place we will all disappear, the earth will be burnt out.

You know all this if you have read the newspapers or talked to certain scientists. It has been like this for the forty-five thousand years that archaeologists and biologists say human beings have existed on this earth: people have struggled, fought, killed. And as it has been before, it shall be now, and that is the future of mankind—everlasting struggle, everlasting quarrels, destruction. This is what you are facing, not only you but your grandchildren. And we accept it. If you are a Jew or a Hindu, you assert that you are a Jew or a Hindu. So we are sustaining, nourishing, the destruction of human beings. This is what is going on, and the politicians cannot solve the problem. On the contrary, they are adding more and more problems. In the very solution of one problem, they multiply a dozen other problems. You can see all this.

Our brains are crowded with problems. If we are aware of what is going on inwardly, we see that we are very primitive people. Though we have lived on this earth for forty-five thousand years, we are very barbarous people, cruel people. We are more or less what we have been from the beginning of time: hating, jealous, frightened; and in our fear we create all kinds of horrors. This is the world in which we live outwardly and inwardly. No philosophy, no guru, no politician, nobody has solved our human problems. You can escape from them by joining some monastery, by taking certain vows or joining some cult, but no authority has ever solved our human problems. We have reached a point where we do not believe in anything. We are utterly confused. Those who are certain at the beginning end up with uncertainty. I start by believing firmly in God or in some kind of mystical affair. If I am somewhat intelligent, as I grow up I begin to doubt everything. One must *begin* with *uncertainty*, doubting, questioning, having a skeptical mind; then one comes to a place where there is absolute certainty.

After all, both outwardly and inwardly we are seeking security. That is why we have invented God, because that is the ultimate security. Don't be shocked, please. Probably the majority believe in God or some higher principle; but all that is invented by thought. Thought is a material process, so anything created by thought in the world of religion is still as materialistic as technology is.

Together we are taking a journey to find out if we human beings can radically bring about a change in ourselves, not through compulsion, not through some enticement or some promise, but because we see things as they are. We see the frightening, desperate state mankind has reached, the confusion that people who really think are in, because we have been told so many contradictory things all through life. We are confused human beings, whether you admit it or not, confused even in the deep layers of consciousness. The world has reached the point where people believe neither in the scientists nor in politicians, nor in any of the thoughtless so-called gurus. Humanity has not changed; but when we have reached this deep stage of confusion, then that very confusion demands right action, that very confusion brings a crisis in our life. The crisis is not out there; the crisis is in our consciousness, in our being.

Is it possible to bring about a deep *psychological* revolution in ourselves, not an outward revolution? The outward revolutions have failed: the recent revolutions. What is important is that there should be a psychological mutation, a fundamental change in the very cells of the brain. The cells in the brain are conditioned. The speaker is not a specialist in the structure of the brain, but he has discussed it with many scientists. One can watch it in oneself, which is much more important than talking to scientists with their authority and contradictions. We can see in ourselves how our brains are conditioned nationally, linguistically, by religion, by economics. Can the cells of that very brain that has been conditioned through knowledge, through education, bring about a mutation in themselves? If someone has been trained as a Muslim, repeating the Koran from childhood, the brain naturally has adjusted itself to the words, to the content of the words, to the meaning of the words and so on, so the brain becomes conditioned by the climate, by the food, by the tradition, by education. So knowledge itself becomes the conditioning factor.

Knowledge is the outcome of experience, and experience and knowledge are limited. After two hundred years of hypotheses, various experiments, scientists have gradually, bit by bit, accumulated a great deal of knowledge about matter. But knowledge is never complete; whether it is knowledge of the Koran or the Bible, it is always limited, because it is based on experience, and experience is always limited. When once you grasp that fact, the reality of that, then you see that *all* thinking is limited. Thinking is the reaction of memory, which is stored in the very cells of the brain, and those cells have been conditioned through centuries of human living and experience and struggle. And we are asking whether those cells themselves can undergo a fundamental mutation so that a human being is entirely different, no longer conditioned. You might say that it is not possible. That would be a natural reaction; we have lived this way for so many centuries, how could that change, how could that mutation take place? It requires a great deal of inquiry, a great deal of attention, energy, passion, to find out. Most of us are lethargic; we are occupied with so many things, occupied with our living, frightened of what is going to happen, frightened of the past, frightened of the future, frightened of the present.

Look at things as they are without any prejudice, without any conclusion. If you have conclusions, opinions, judgments, put them aside because it is only a brain that is free that can look. Can you put aside all opinions, judgments, evaluation, tradition, and look at things as they are? Not as a politician, not as a foreigner, not as a person who has read a great deal and can speak endlessly, but as a human being? Our brains are conditioned to solve problems, so the brain itself has a problem, and therefore whatever it meets turns into a problem. Is it possible not to have a brain that is conditioned to the solution of problems; to have a brain that is free to look and not make a problem of what it looks at? Can the brain cells themselves, without any compulsion, without any instigation, without any pressure, outwardly or inwardly, bring about a change, a mutation in themselves?

Religion is the most important thing in life. A new culture, a new civilization, cannot come about through economic adjustments, political action, through various forms of institutions and foundations. Religion is the only factor. Our inquiry is to find out whether the human brain can be really religious. We mean, by *religion*, absolute freedom: freedom from fear, freedom from conflict, freedom from problems, freedom from sorrow, so that a brain is completely free. It is only then that there is the quality of love and compassion. That state alone can find out what is sacred. And in the understanding of that truth, in the perception of that which is true, there is peace, peace in oneself, in one's own psyche. That means no conflict whatsoever.

Now is this possible? If you say it is not possible, then that becomes a block that prevents you from looking at the possibility of opening the door to look. Or if you say it *is* possible, then you are merely talking theoretically, then you have shut the door. So you must have the quality of a brain that is inquiring, looking, searching, asking, questioning, doubting.

Not only doubting others, your books and so on, but doubting your own thinking, questioning your own responses, your own reactions. That requires an alertness of mind.

The first thing we are asking is: what is thinking? We live by thinking. All our actions are based on thinking; our relationship with each other is part of thinking; the images that you have built about your wife or your husband, your guru, your leaders, and so on, are put together by thought as an image. Thinking is our fundamental instrument. We may think devotionally, romantically, imaginatively, but it is still thinking. A scientist, a philosopher, mathematician, biologist, or just an ordinary human being, even the most uneducated person, thinks. So our first inquiry is to find out what thinking is, why thinking has become so extraordinarily important.

We must understand very clearly the nature of our thinking. Please observe your own thinking. Observe your own thoughts, how they arise, how limited they are. Each one of us is concerned about himself; basically, we are self-centered though we may try to hide it behind all kinds of words. And that self-centered thinking is limited. When you think about yourself, your achievements, your desires, your purposes, it is still limited. Whatever is limited must bring about conflict, must bring about division. That's a law. If I am divided against you, thinking about myself all day long, it is a very limited process. That's what we are all doing; happily, miserably, successfully, that is what we are doing. So thinking, being limited, has made our whole outlook limited. Because it is limited, it has created nationalities, hoping to find security in tribalism, in tribal gods. And you haven't found security. You thought there would be security in communities, but there has been no security there either. So where is security? Where is security for us? It is not through division, not through labeling oneself.

What will make us change? We have had sorrow, pain; we have had wars, every kind of toil and travail; and yet we go on as we are. What will make us change? Reward? Reward in heaven, reward on this earth? When you are seeking for a reward there is always the other side of it, punishment. Reward and punishment is one of our principles. So it becomes very important to find out if thought—which has created such havoc in the world—is the only instrument that we have.

Scientists have produced not only medicine and surgery and fast communication, and those happy, convenient things, but also they have produced most diabolical things: nuclear war, nuclear instruments, the atom bomb, the submarine. The whole technological world of warfare is the product of thought. Going to the moon is a product of thought. And putting a flag up there is a product of thought! Our relationship with each other is based on thought.

You are related. Life is a process of relationship. Living is relationship. You cannot possibly live by yourself; even though you may retire for the rest of your life to the Himalayas or to a community or to a monastery, you are still in contact with humanity, you are related. You may not be related to a person, but you are related to a tradition, related to knowledge, related to all kinds of things. So relationship is one of the basic factors of life: husband and wife and children in relationship, with their conflicts, with their sexual demands, with their pleasures, with their pains, with their flattery, with their insults, with their nagging. You know all that goes on in relationship. In that relationship you have created—thought has created—the image about your wife, and your wife has created an image about you. That's a fact. And the relationship is between these two images. The husband says, "I know my wife," and the wife says, "I know my husband," but you really don't know each other. All that you know is the image you have about her, and she has an image about you. That is built through time. Where the relationship is between two images, there is actually no relationship at all. That's again a fact. And that is why there is such conflict in relationship. There are very few people living together who are really related, happy, not adjusting to each other, or tolerating each other, or exploiting each other.

So, is it possible to live without a single image? Who is it who creates the images? You are sitting there, and you have an image about me, haven't you? The image that you have built about me is not me. Some people worship that image. You may not worship it, you might kick it aside or disregard it, but still you have created an image about me, so your relationship is with the image and not with me at all.

To have a relationship, we must meet each other at the same level, at the same time, with the same intensity. Isn't that love? When you meet somebody at the same level, at the same time, with the same intensity—not sexually, I am not talking of that—but with all your human being, with your whole being, then that is love. And there is no love if you have images about each other. And where there is love, there is no time. Where there is love, there is no conflict. And to understand that extraordinary thing called love you must have great intelligence; and not fear, not ambition, not greed, not jealousy, not hatred.

As our brains are conditioned by thought, through thought, which is the activity of time, a material process, is it possible to find a totally different movement that is not of thought, that is not put together by thought? If thought is the only instrument we have, we are condemned for ever, because then all our action becomes limited. Then whatever we do, religiously, politically, economically, will always be limited and therefore cause perpetual conflict and more problems. Thought is necessary, but is thought necessary in relationship with each other?

To discover for oneself a process of living in which thought doesn't come in requires enormous inquiry. This requires a great deal of your attention, because knowledge has become so important to you. Truth is not knowledge, it is not something put together by thought, it is something that comes into being when the brain is totally free, uncontaminated, pristine, original. And to discover that is part of meditation—which is not stupid repetition.

We are not talking about something theoretical, hypothetical. We are dealing with facts. Facts are what is happening now, what has happened before, not what is going to happen. The fact is what you are thinking, doing now, and the fact of what you have done before. Those are facts. But ideals are not facts. You have ideals, so you live in illusory worlds. When your brain lives in an illusory world, you are bound to create conflict for yourself and for others. Your opinion, like any other opinion, is not a fact. But what you do out of that opinion, out of that conclusion, out of that theory, is a fact. If you have an illusion and act according to that illusion, that becomes a fact, and that you have an illusion is a fact, too.

Will you question all authority, your own authority first, and the authority of your religion, of your gods, of your temples? Question the politicians, question everything, doubt so that your own brain begins to be active.

Humility can come naturally, uninvited, easily, only when you begin to question your own thoughts, your own relationship, your own desires, your own achievements. Out of that comes the quality of humility. When there is humility, you are then learning. Learning is infinite; knowledge is limited. Bowing down to somebody is not humility. Humility is saying, "I don't know, let's find out." It is to be free to look and to have great simplicity, not the simplicity of a loincloth but the simplicity of a clear mind and clear heart.

Then only does that which is beyond time come into being.

10

A Dimension That Is Not
the Invention of Thought

W HY CAN'T WE LIVE with each other, intimately or otherwise, with tranquillity, a certain quality of serenity?
We have been talking about whether we can in our daily life
end conflict within ourselves, be free of any shadow of fear,
end suffering, and move away entirely from the self-centered
activity that is, or is one of the major causes of, conflict, not
only outwardly but also inwardly. Very few seem to be serious
enough to go into this deeply and perhaps realize that there is
a totally different way of living. Why has humanity become
what it is? Is it our inevitable lot to live this way? Has something gone wrong with the whole human evolution? Is there
something outside, beyond human measure, that if one can understand, go into it deeply, may perhaps open the door, open
our eyes and perhaps our hearts too, so that we may naturally,
easily, live a happy, serene life?

We must understand the word *experience*. Experience
is a process of acquiring knowledge, becoming familiar with
something. And knowledge may be one of the fundamental
reasons for our conflict, our ignorance. Not technological, scientific, and medical knowledge, and so on, but the accumulated

knowledge of humanity, which is the whole burden of the past, may be one of the basic causes of conflict.

Is there is an outside agency, beyond the measure of man, beyond man himself, that we can appeal to, pray to, ask for guidance, or be with so basically that we are that, so that there is no outside agency? Or, is a human being the measure of all things? A human being is our consciousness, reactions, memories. Is that the measure, or is there something outside of us that, if we can come into contact with it, may help us? This has been the activity of religion. Throughout the world, from ancient days, people have sought something outside. Or we have said there is something divine in the human, but it is covered over with greed, with envy, with ambitions and cruelty, bestiality, and, if that can be stripped away, then there will be the abiding factor of righteous behavior. To strip away all the layers of our ugly, brutal, anxious, ambitious, aggressive life, there have been many, many systems, many incantations, many forms of rituals, magic. We have tried every form of physical torture—fasting, denying every sensory response—to come to the point where we can understand and live a different way of life. Scientists are also trying, through genetic engineering, through chemistry, drugs, to change man. People have looked in every direction outwardly, and perhaps never inwardly. We may have superficially scratched the surface of our existence, but have not, except for a few, been deeply concerned and gone into ourselves. We are both matter and the movement of thought, which is also matter. The instrument of investigation to go into ourselves has been thought—and thought is not the right instrument, because thought itself is limited.

Religions throughout the world, organized and not organized, individuals and groups, have made every form of attempt to become enlightened—to use that word that has been so corrupted by the gurus. Can we put aside all the religious dogmas, faiths, systems, symbols, figures, rituals, and not belong to any group, to any spiritual authority. Those two words *spiritual authority* are the denial of spirituality. Could we slough off all that to stand completely free, unafraid, so that we can inquire into the actual, to see if there is a dimension that is not the invention of thought?

What is the origin, the beginning of all existence, from the most minute cell to the most complex brain? Was there a beginning at all, and is there an end to all this? We are going to inquire together into what creation is. To find all this, to uncover all this, what kind of brain does one need? What kind of capacity, what kind of energy, what kind of passion is needed to really probe into all of this? To probe into something totally unknown, not preconceived, not caught in any sentimental, romantic illusion, there must be a quality of brain that is completely free—free from all its conditioning, from all its programming, from every kind of influence, and therefore highly sensitive and tremendously active. Is that possible? Do you have such a brain? Or is it very sluggish, lazy and living in its own self-conceit? Which is it? To inquire into this demands a mind, a brain, that is extraordinarily alive, not caught in any form of mechanical routine. Is that possible?

Do we have a brain in which there is no fear, no self-interest, no self-centered activity? Otherwise it is living in its own shadow all the time. It is living in its own tribal, limited environment, field. It is like an animal tied to a stake; the tether may be very long or very short, but it is tied to a post so its movement is limited. You may give it a very long rope, but the very length is an indication of limitation.

A brain must have space. So what is space? Not only the space between here and there, but space without a center. If you have a center, and you move away from the center to the periphery, however far away the periphery is, it is still limited. Space where there is no center has no periphery; there is no boundary. Have we such a brain so that we do not belong to anything, are not attached to anything, are not attached to our experiences, conclusions, hopes, ideals, and so on, so that the brain is really, completely free? If it is burdened, you cannot go very far. If it is crude, vulgar, self-centered, it cannot have measureless space. And space indicates—one is using the word very, very carefully—emptiness.

We are trying to find out if it is possible to live in this world without any fear, without any conflict, with a tremendous sense of compassion, which demands a great deal of intelligence. You cannot have compassion without intelligence. And that intelligence is not the activity of thought. One cannot be compassionate if one is attached to a particular ideology, to a particular narrow tribalism, or to any religious concept, because that limits. Compassion can come, or be there, only when there is the ending of sorrow, which is the ending of self-centered movement.

Space indicates emptiness, nothingness. And because there is not a thing put there by thought, that space has tremendous energy. The brain must have the quality of complete freedom and space. That is, one must be nothing. Whereas we are all something; we are analysts, psychotherapists, doctors. That is all right, but when we are therapists, when we are biologists, technicians, that very identification limits the wholeness of the brain.

Only then can we ask what meditation is. There are many forms of meditation, systems of meditation; they are all based on making thought silent, making thought quiet, not having thought rampant. That is, there is a controller who is going to control through a system, through practice, through a daily allotted time for quietness, and so on. There is always the controller watching. And the controller itself is the activity of thought. So they are going round and round in a circle like a cat chasing its own tail. And that is called meditation.

Now, meditation is something entirely different. If the house is not in order, meditation has very little meaning: there cannot be order if there is fear; there cannot be order if there is any kind of conflict. You can invent any kind of illusion, any kind of enlightenment, any kind of daily discipline; it will still be limited, illusory, because it is born out of disorder. Only when our inward house is in complete order, so there is great stability with great strength in that very stability, that one can ask what true meditation is. Unless there is this kind of *undisciplined order*, meditation becomes very shallow and meaningless.

So then, what is order? Thought cannot create order, because thought itself is disorder, because thought is based on knowledge, which is based on experience. All knowledge is limited, and so thought is also limited. And when thought tries to create order, it brings about disorder. This is actual fact, not theory. Thought has created disorder through conflict between *what is* and *what should be*, the actual and the theoretical. But there is only the actual and not the theoretical. Thought looks at the actual from a limited point of view, and therefore its action must inevitably create disorder.

Suppose I am greedy, envious. That is *what is*; the opposite is not. But the opposite has been created by human beings, by thought as a means of understanding *what is*, and also as a means of escaping from *what is*. There is only *what is*; and when you perceive *what is* without its opposite, then that very perception brings order.

As we were saying, our house must be in order, and this order cannot be brought about by thought. Thought creates its own discipline—do this, don't do that, follow this, don't follow that, be traditional or not traditional, and so on. Thought is the guide. One hopes to bring about order, but thought itself is limited, therefore it is bound to create disorder. If I keep repeating, "I am British or French, or a Hindu or a Buddhist," that tribalism is very limited. And that tribalism is causing great havoc in the world. We don't go to the root of it to end tribalism, instead of seeing how to create better wars. Order can come into being only when thought, which is necessary in certain areas, has no place in the psychological world. That world itself is in order when thought is absent.

The word *meditation* means to measure—to measure between *what is* and *what should be*, between what I am and what I will be through meditation. *Meditation*, in Sanskrit and Latin, means quality of measurement, which is comparison. And comparison is disorder. When I am comparing myself with you, which is competing with you, I am trying to be better than you; then that is a constant conflict, isn't it? So is it possible to live without any comparison, not only biologically, physically, but much more psychologically, inwardly, never comparing oneself with anything, with anybody, so that the mind, the brain, is free from this conflict of arrogance?

What is meditation? It is necessary to have a brain that is absolutely quiet. The brain has its own rhythm. One has watched all this in oneself; which doesn't mean that the speaker is extraordinary. Don't let's become sentimental and personal. The brain is endlessly active, chattering from one subject to another, from one thought to another, from one association to another, from one state to another. It is constantly occupied. One is not aware of it generally; but when one is aware without any choice, choicelessly aware of this movement, then that very awareness, that very attention, ends the chattering. Please do it, and you will see how simple it all is.

So the quality of the brain must be free, must have space and silence psychologically. You and I talk to each other. There, thought is being employed because we are speaking English. But to speak out of silence....

This brings the question of language. Does language condition the brain? Have you ever thought about all this? Or is it all something totally new? Does English or French or whatever, Russian or Chinese, does the very usage of language shape the brain so that it becomes conditioned? Language does condition the brain. If you talk to a Russian or to a Frenchman, someone British or American, their whole outlook is limited by the language they use. Can we be free of the network of words, use a language like English and not allow it to shape our outlook on the whole of existence?

If you have not done any of these things, it is all something fanciful. Not to be caught in the network of words is also quite complex. When you say, "I am a communist," your whole reaction is different; the label is more important than the person. So there must be freedom from the word. Then the brain is utterly quiet, though it has its own rhythm.

Now, then, what is creation, what is the beginning of all this? We are inquiring into the origin, the beginning of all life; not only our life, but the life of every living thing—the whales in the deep, the dolphins, the little fish, the vast nature, the beauty of a tiger, and the living of human beings, from the most minute cells to the most complex person, with all our inventions, with all our illusions, with our superstitions, with our quarrels, with our wars, with our arrogance, vulgarity, with our tremendous aspirations and our great depressions. What is the origin of all this?

Now, meditation is to come upon this—not *you* come upon it. In that silence, in that quietness, in that absolute tranquillity, is there a beginning? And if there is a beginning, there must be an ending. That which has a cause must end. Wherever there is a cause, there must be an end. That is a law, that is natural. So is there a causation at all for the creation of humanity, the creation of all the way of life? Is there a beginning of all this? How are we going to find out?

Religions have said there is God, that God is the beginning and the end of all things. That is a very easy way of solving the problem. The Hindus have said it in one way, perhaps the Buddhists, too, and Christianity said, "God." The fundamentalists believe that man was created 4,500 years ago. It seems rather absurd because 4,500 years ago, the Egyptians invented the calendar, which means they must have been extraordinarily advanced. If you are a fundamentalist, then you'll get angry with what is being said. I hope none of us is any kind of fundamentalist.

So what is creation? Not the painter who creates the picture, not the poet, not the man who makes something out of marble? Those are all things manifested. Is there something which is not manifested? Is there something, because it is not manifested, that has no beginning and no end? That which is manifested has a beginning, has an end. We are the manifestations, aren't we? Not of divine something or other; we are the result of thousands of years of so-called evolution, growth, development; and we also come to an end. That which is manifested can always be destroyed—but that which is not has no time.

Now we are asking if there is something beyond all time. This has been the inquiry of philosophers, scientists, and religious people, to find that which is beyond the measure of man, which is beyond time. Because if one can find, come upon, discover that, or see that, that is immortality. That is beyond death. Human beings have sought this in various ways, in different parts of the world, through different beliefs. Because when one discovers that, or realizes that, life then has no beginning and no end. Therefore it is beyond all concepts, beyond all hope. It is something immense.

Now, to come back to earth. You see, we never look at our own life as a tremendous wide movement with a great depth, a vastness. We have reduced our life to such a shoddy little affair. And life is really the most sacred thing in existence. To kill somebody is the most irreligious horror. To get angry, to be violent with somebody . . . the speaker has been angry only once and the person with whom he was angry has been reminding him, still carrying on with the anger.

You see, we never see the world as a whole because we are so fragmented, we are so terribly limited, so petty. We never have the feeling of wholeness, where the things of the sea, things of the earth, nature and the sky, the universe, are part of us. This is not imagined. You can go off into some kind of fanciful imagination and imagine that you are the universe, then you become cuckoo! But, to break down this small, self-centered interest, to have nothing of that, then from there you can move infinitely.

And meditation is this. Not sitting cross-legged, or standing on your head, or doing whatever one does, but to have this feeling of complete wholeness and unity of life. And that can come only when there is love and compassion.

You know, one of our difficulties is that we have associated love with pleasure, with sex. And love also, for most of us, means jealousy, anxiety, possessiveness, attachment. That is what we call love. So is love attachment? Is love pleasure? Is love desire? Is love the opposite of hate? If it is the opposite of hate, then it is not love. All opposites contain their own opposites. When I try to become courageous, that courage is born out of fear. So love cannot have its opposite. Love cannot be where there is jealousy, ambition, aggressiveness.

And where there is that quality, then from that arises compassion. Where there is that compassion, there is intelligence. Not the intelligence of self-interest, not the intelligence of thought, not the intelligence of a great deal of knowledge. Compassion has nothing to do with knowledge. Only compassion is that intelligence which gives humanity security, stability, a vast sense of strength.

Sources

THIS BOOK IS DRAWN FROM THE FOLLOWING TALKS:

"Putting Our House in Order." New Delhi, India, November 6, 1983.

"Where Can We Find Peace?" Saanen, Switzerland, July 10, 1983.

"Thought and Knowledge Are Limited." Ojai, California, May 14, 1983.

"War Is a Symptom." Ojai, California, May 15, 1983.

"The Narrow Circle of the Self." Saanen, Switzerland, July 12, 1983.

"Can the Brain Be Totally Free?" Brockwood Park, England, August 27, 1983.

"Consciousness Is Shared by All Human Beings." Brockwood Park, England, August 28, 1983.

"Suffering and Death." Brockwood Park, England, September 3, 1983.

"In the Perception of What Is True There Is Peace." Madras (Chennai), India, December 31, 1983.

"A Dimension That Is Not the Invention of Thought." Brockwood Park, England, September 4, 1983.